OF ZOOM, FRIENDS & CATS

WINTER 2020

THE EXPANSION PACK

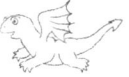

CONTENTS

Paperback ISBN # 978-1-64820-006-9

First paperback edition February 2021.

Published by Idalium Books in the U.S.A.

Idalium Books
NOW Nation Publications
P.O. Box 796582
Dallas, TX 75379-9998

321 Purr Street
New Development Hall
Cambridge, MA 02138

To THE READERS of The Expansion Pack: Of Zoom, Friends & Cats:

I am writing to express my strong support of The Expansion Pack (TXP) — an open-minded community — for selection in *The Great Group of Friends* fellowship.

I was introduced to members of TXP, starting in April 2019 when I entered an online community program.

As the group changed, several outstanding and accomplished members took the opportunity to gain hands-on experience and deliver independent and committed support with uncompromising ethical integrity. Thus, TXP officially launched in September 2020.

Since the launch, TXP members have been invited to write and share an introduction about themselves. This process was unexpectedly and humbly completed with great success in December 2020, paving the way for TXP to grow, and for new members to share themselves in a similar vein.

It was clear from the very first week that TXP was truly an intellectually-engaged community, providing outstanding social support. An insightful and well-structured quarterly planning process was promptly organized, and completed with exceptional turnout.

Furthermore, TXP provides ongoing support though weekly accountability, as well as in daily work-cycle activities. TXP also hosts social gatherings and other activities through the suggestion and advocacy of groups of readers, writers, and doodling enthusiasts. These are just a few examples of many, which illustrate TXP's outstanding and powerful resourcefulness and the depth of its members' intellectual curiosity.

While providing support to others, TXP also develops plans for independent projects, and quickly became active in experimenting with strategies to create new opportunities. In the fall of 2020, TXP already launched several creative pursuits, for example, by completing and publishing a book.

In addition to gaining experience with creating, TXP is learning how to navigate the challenges of co-creating. This further illustrates TXP's strong interest in interactions between members, and how challenges are relished. TXP is ambitious, fast-evolving, curious about by the power of belonging, and fascinated by different ways of thinking.

Even though TXP had no prior background, it quickly became proficient in fulfilling the juxtaposing desires of introspection and social engagement, and provided a strong foundation of integrity, trust, and acceptance with an energetic and encouraging space for its members to move out of their comfort zones.

TXP bears witness to transformation and growth, and delights in seeing its members flourish.

I would like to restate my strongest support and recommend TXP with the highest confidence.

Sincerely yours,

Director Z.
Center for Community Involvement
Department of Cat Allies

Ĝi kredas, ke vi estas granda, stulta, kalva kat',
Kaj tuj superruzita de la muso kaj la rat',
Pensante, ke vi certe mortos baldaŭ pro malsat',
Ĝi lasas ĉiutage mortan korpon sur la mat'.

"Vi estas tro diabla!" *'Vi estas nekapabla.*
Vi mortos pro malsato,' diras ĝi.
"Mi sentas min ne ema..." *'Vi estas nedankema!*
Mi lasis ĝian kapon, nur por vi!'

Matene vi manĝigas, tamen poste, ĉiam ĝi
rigardas vin dum vi tagmanĝas kun la famili',
"Ho, ne! Malbona kato! Vi ne ŝtelu tion ĉi!"
Sed jam ĝi malaperis, tro rapide, eĉ por vi.

Sed kiam vi kuiras, la kato reeniras,
"Mi certas, ke mi jam manĝigis vin..."
Ĝi kuras ĝis telero, *'FROMAJXA HAMBURGERO?!*
MI PETI CXU MI RAJTAS HAVAS GXI?>!>?!'

Kaj kiam vi ricevas pakojn, prepariĝu tuj,
Batalo komenciĝos pri skatolo (aŭ "katuj'"),
Ĝi gratos vin kaj kuros for, dum vi kriegas, "Huj!"
Vi trovos ĝin dormante iam poste en lavuj'.

'Se estas laŭmezure, sidiĝas mi plezure!'
Vi provas forfikigi ĝin per ĵet',
Sed kia malakordo! Ĝi saltas tra la pordo,
Kaj puŝas ĉiujn aĵojn for de l' bret'.

Senmove, ĝi eksteren fiksrigardas, kiam vi
malfermas vian pordon centafoje, pli malpli,
Ĝi sidas, pripensante, sur ŝtupar'—"Sed kio pri?"
'Ĉu homoj surteriĝas stare? Ĉu kontrolu mi?'

Kaj sur ŝtelita seĝo, ĝi sidas kiel reĝo,
Aŭ kuŝas ĝi senzorge sur klavar',
Aŭ frue la matenon, ĝi grimpas la kurtenon,
Aŭ vekas vin per piso en harar'.

Komprenu, ke ekzistas multaj pli ol tiuj por
nemiam havi katon (aŭ por ĝin irigi for),
Laŭ mi, ne estas grave; malgraŭ tiu ĉi dolor',
Mi amas miajn katojn—per mia tuta kor'. ♥

- decembro 2020

CHAPTER 3

VARIOUS REASONS TO NEVER HAVE A CAT (A VERY APPROXIMATE ENGLISH TRANSLATION)

BY SQUIDDIE

He thinks you're just a giant, stupid, useless, hairless cat,
Who's easily outwitted by a little mouse or rat,
Believing that you'll starve to death, in spite of being fat,
Each day he leaves a dead or dying rodent on the mat.

"You absolute disgrace!" *'You total waste of space.*
You'll die from malnutrition—quickly, too.'
"You know, that isn't food..." *'You're being kind of rude!*
I left the head especially for you!'

You feed him every morning, yet he always asks for more,
He watches while you're eating, sniffing crumbs upon the floor,
"That bloody cat! It took my fish! Get back here—this means war!"
Before you've finished swearing, he's already out the door.

But later when you're cooking, he wanders back in, looking,
And sees your food: *'IZ BURGER MADE WIZ CHEEZ?!'*
"You think that I'd forget? You literally just ate!"
'MOAR HUNGERS NOW SO I CAN HAS IT PLZ?>!>?!'

Whenever you receive a package, brace for the affray
that certainly will follow if you take the box away,
He'll hiss and bite and scratch your eyes and bolt as you shout,
"Hey!"
You'll find him sleeping in the sink much later in the day.

'Wherever I can fits, I has the right for sits!'
You curse and brusquely throw him out the door,
He takes it on himself to jump up on the shelf,
And push all of your things onto the floor.

He's staring out the door for what must be, without a doubt,
the hundredth time you've opened it—you fight the urge to shout,
Then sitting on the stairs, he's deep in thought—"But what about?"
'Do people land upon their feet? Perhaps I should find out?'

He sits, with regal air, upon a stolen chair,
Or on your keyboard while he licks his balls,
He'll wake you up, for certain, by climbing up the curtain,
Or sitting on your head when nature calls.

I'm sure you've guessed that all these things are only just the start
of reasons not to get a cat (or make your cat depart),
The truth is I'm just joking—cats are friendly, sweet and smart!
I love my cats so dearly, from the bottom of my heart. ♥

- December 2020

We have all heard snazzy quotes like, "you get what you negotiate," "you get what you tolerate," "you get what you wish for," or my favorite, "you get what you deserve." I believed that one for the longest time, but it's not the whole story.

All of these aphorisms have some truth to them. In some situations, they work very well. But most of them work only in the short run.

They can be useful to keep in mind at different times and phases of our lives.

For example, when I was working as a software engineer, I truly believed that we get what we deserve and that my manager would notice my efforts and do everything to help me get what I worked for. But instead, my manager gave me a hard time for a while.

At that time, it was constructive to remind myself that "I get what I negotiate." I negotiated hard and got a rating three levels higher than what they had intended to give me. The initial rating they intended to provide was "meets most expectations". I ended up getting "strongly exceeds expectations", just below the best possible rating of "redefines expectations".

"I got what I negotiated for" is not the whole truth, however. It seemed like the answer when I had worked hard but not asked for the appropriate fruits of my labor. If I had changed my strategy to just negotiate for the next few years while the quality of my work slipped, I don't think it would have worked very well in the long run.

Here are the things I have learned about *how* we get what we get.

We get what we work *and* ask for

The "and" is the key here. Both sides of the equation are essential.

We tend to focus on extremes because they are useful from time to time and easy to back up with evidence and anecdotes.

For example, silence is effective sometimes, and words are effective at other times. It's easier to illustrate times when one or the other was the correct choice than to explain how they each have their time to shine.

But if we want to tease out some principles from our experiences, things are much more complicated. That is where the middle path is helpful.

The answers to many "yes-no" questions about life turn out to be "it depends."

I love middle paths. They accept and celebrate the nuances and complexity of life.

The middle path

Bo Lozoff, in his book *It's a Meaningful Life, It Just Takes Practice*, points out:

"The cause of all our personal problems and nearly all the problems of the world can be summed up in a single sentence: Human life is very deep, and our modern dominant lifestyle is not."

Even if we don't believe this is the cause of all problems, we can see that approaching things from a shallow and simplistic perspective causes oscillations in our life. We keep going to extremes, only to realize that they only work for a short time.

One way to approach the middle path is to find a continuum between discrete points. We tend to see things in black and white, 0 or 1, binary. But there is always the color to things, even if it's just grayscale. One day, in graduate school, I was reading a paper that assumed the population was either selfish or altruistic and did some derivations based on that. I wanted to add a degree of selfishness to that model: in essence, not assuming that something is 0 (selfish) or altruistic (1), but a continuum in between—the middle path. Approaching the problem from a continuum angle led us to publish a paper about network routing games[1] in which we introduced a dial of selfishness that let us fine tune what fraction of people are selfish.

In real life too, there are dials for any quality. Both extremes help in different situations. It is the middle path that is the balanced person.

When things seem simple, there is almost always a deeper layer of understanding waiting to be found in the middle path.

You get what you work for AND what you ask for — through the middle path

Now back to my belief:

You get what you work for *and* what you ask for.

You get success if you work for it and also ask for it.

You get happiness if you work for it and also ask for it.

If I do both, then things do work out for me.

"Working" is about putting in the work to deliver good value. "Asking" is about presenting the value to the relevant people, "selling the idea," and asking for a reward.

Without putting in the work, selling can work only for so long.

Without asking, people might not appreciate what you have put work into, reducing the likelihood of your reward.

Sometimes, people who are strong on the "working" side get jealous of people who are good at the "asking" side. They start to believe that the world is unfair and you only need to be assertive and sell in order to win. In practice though, we humans feel insecure if we get things we have not worked for. We might feel good in the short run, but eventually, we feel guilty and unhappy. It is not a recipe for long term success. Eventually the well runs dry, if you don't replenish it with hard work.

On the other hand, if you don't ask for things, you are unlikely to get the rewards you are looking for. You might not even know what reward you are looking for. Certainly, what you are looking for is not clear to others.

Some people look for a promotion as a reward for hard work in their jobs. For others, money and compensation are more important. For even others, it is the recognition that matters. So, if we don't ask for our reward, we might get what we are not looking for.

Here is an apt example:

I was working with someone last year who was working enough for a role two positions above theirs, but they had a really hard time asking for the promotion they wanted.

A few months of deeper exploration and exercises lead them to asking, and they got the promotion almost immediately. That is the power of asking.

"Asking" as described here is very broad. It is about letting the relevant parties know what you worked for and what you want.

Sometimes, it can be via speaking about your work. Other times, it might be via showcasing your work. It might involve showing off the features of the product you are building, not the intricate details, in order to win over people unfamiliar with your area of expertise and help them adopt the product.

When I first realized that I need to ask for things in order to get them, I was very frustrated. Why can't my manager or other someone else just give me my reward?

A friend of mine put the "asking" exercise in perspective when he told me: *selling your work is a way of being honest*. If we are not selling, we probably believe the value to be whatever we make up in our heads. But if we are selling, we need to agree on the value and impact with entities outside of our head. The world has a way of keeping us honest.

If we work hard, we must share the results with those who can reward us to assign value together and thereby, get what we deserve.

Other dichotomies

The two activities we talked about on the path to success are "working" and "asking". The way these look vary in different arenas.

• If you are presenting something to influence someone, your content has to be good (working), but presentation and body language are also important (asking).

• If you are building a product, the product itself needs to be high quality for it to be successful (working), but your marketing and sales efforts will determine the ultimate success (asking).

• For a movie to be a success, it has to be good (working), but if the trailer is no good (asking), people might never watch it.

In short, you have to get the details right, be clear about what you are looking for, and ask for it.

When you are the one who is making other people successful

So far, we have approached this topic from the point of view of the person looking for rewards. But it can be helpful to visualize yourself as your own customer or manager by thinking about a time when the roles are reversed. It feels reasonable when someone else works for and asks for your resources, so why think of it as unreasonable to do so yourself?

Imagine somebody is selling courses online, and you buy one. What will make you buy from (reward) the same person again?

• The content of the course has to be good. If it is not, you might be fooled into buying repeatedly. The trust will break pretty quickly if the content starts to suffer.

• The person has to ask for your attention and your money to be successful. Without that, you might have never heard of the course. Their marketing can be all word of mouth, but they still have to ask people to buy. If they never ask for a sale (e.g., offering paid content), they will never get the sale.

Your turn

To see in your own life how you need both the "working" and "asking" part in order to earn what you are looking for, I have a short exercise for you, to answer the following questions:

• What is one project or area of your life where you are working for rewards, but not asking for them? Once you identify this project or area, what can you ask for? From whom?

• What is one area where you are asking for more than you are actually earning? It can be hard to recognize such an area, especially if it goes against our values to do so, but it is worth digging deep and seeing if there is anything there. What more can you do in this area to deserve what you are getting?

---

1. https://www.sciencedirect.com/science/article/abs/pii/S0899825609001298

It's taking over
It's like a weight on the atmosphere
Pushing everything down
The force is enormous
What can I do but to give in?

I'm well aware
That I want to give in
Let it rule both me
And my whole experience
For a while

Sometimes that while is long
Much longer that you'd think
But why not just let it go on
When the whole world
Is waiting for you
Then why not let it go on
For yet another while

A short visit to the surface
Just to realize
We are leaving again
That I'll be chanceless
Completely chanceless
Unless I break the spell with force

And they are countless,
The dreams
Perhaps not always seamlessly linked
But so brutally unoffended by that fact
To the point where the experience
Is seamless in the end
It really is

Wait, seams in paradise?
What are you talking about at all?
There's been as many disturbing seams
In these dreams
As has ever been seen
In clusters of clouds
Moving rapidly across the sky

I even reach out sometimes
Thinking that I can touch something
There in the dream
To soon become aware
I'm gripping in air
But they just must be here
They cannot be this real
And at the same time not be here

And heaven, the bliss
When the dreams lead me up
And the curtain goes down
A moment of everything
As well as of nothing
Most of all
It's a moment in my experience

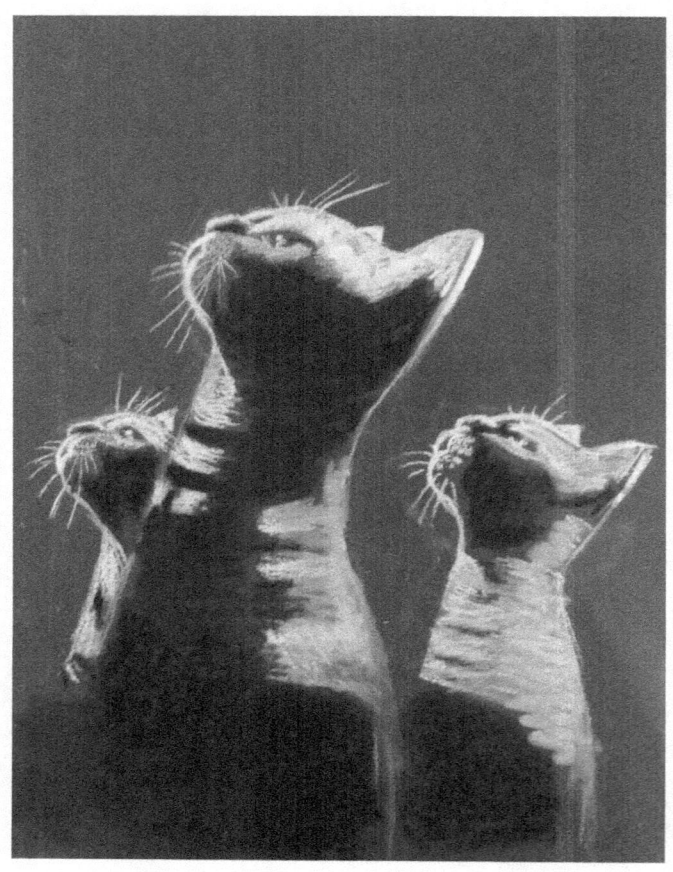

White Cats by Lina Wahlund

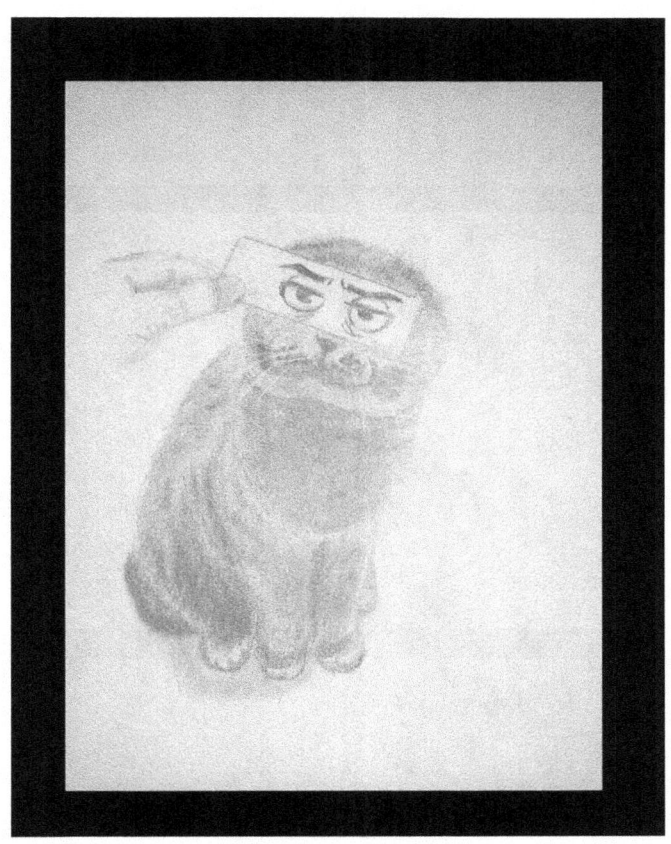

Cool Cat by Lina Wahlund

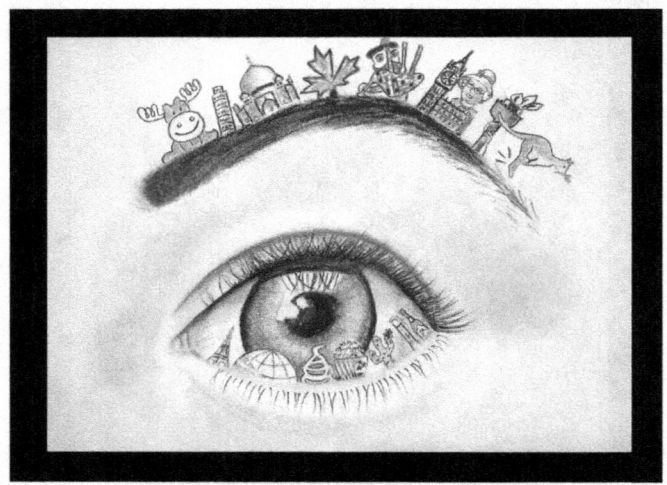

TXP Around the World by Lina Wahlund

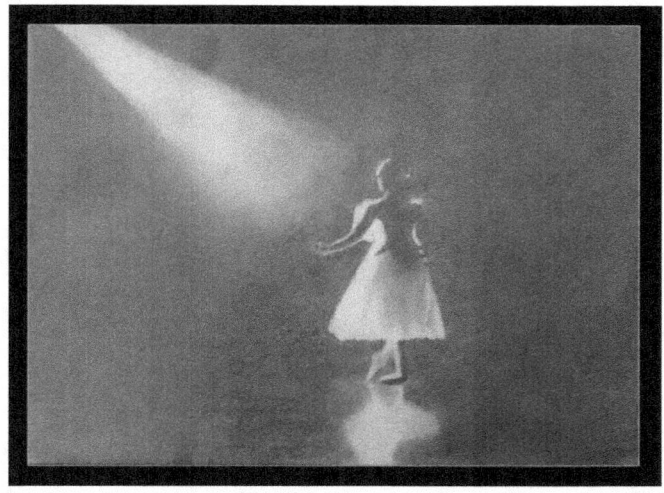

Dancing by Lina Wahlund

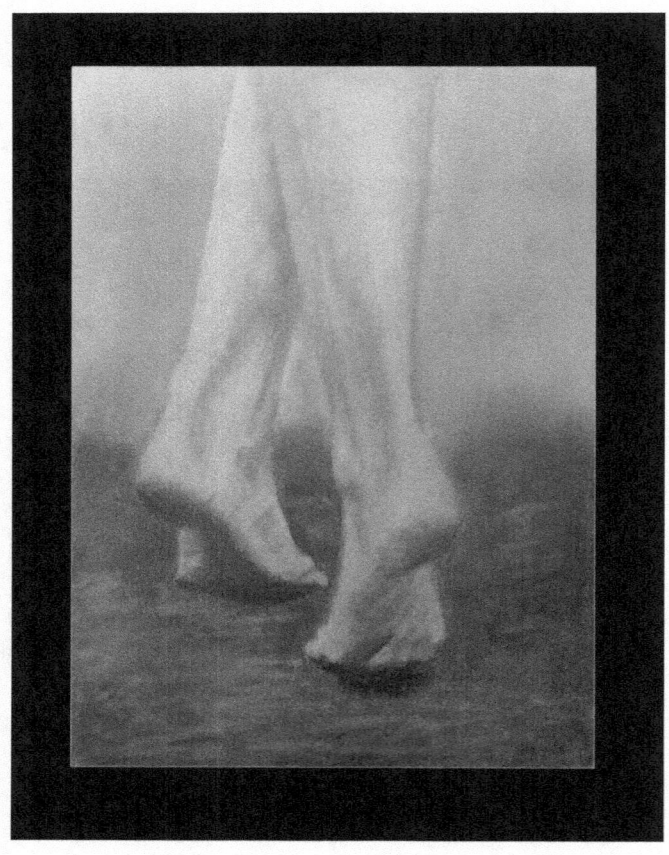

Feet Walking by Lina Wahlund

CHAPTER 6
WHAT IF …?

BY ERIC T.

WHAT IF:

- You sent someone a random message, card, or e-mail of sincere appreciation, and and it reached her just as she was having an especially difficult day and was feeling really down on herself?
- You came up with your own personal menu of ways to put small pockets of free time to positive use, and started implementing them on a daily basis?
- You decided to do the thing you're afraid to do?
- Today ended up being the last day of your life?
- You paused right before you were about to react out of anger, and waited until you were in a better frame of mind to respond?
- You made taking care of yourself a priority?
- It turns out it was much easier than you thought to do something you wanted to do?
- All you had to do was ask?

- You stopped worrying about doing it perfectly, and did it anyway so that others might still benefit?
- You started paying attention to every good thing that happens to you, and wrote these down in a notebook each day?
- It turns out you were wrong?
- It turns out you were right?
- You have other options?
- You already have everything you need?
- You have the power to affect and influence people to a much greater degree than you ever imagined?
- You really showed up for each day?
- You substituted water for soda every day for the rest of your life?
- Taking the risk paid off?
- You didn't get what you thought you wanted, but you still want what you ended up getting?
- One person's life was made easier by something you did today?
- You don't need 50% of the things you spend money on, and could be just as happy without them?
- You started a blog, or a podcast, or a YouTube channel?
- You didn't watch TV for a month, and ended up not missing it?
- You stopped caring what other people might think?
- You did something you previously thought you could never do?
- You took the first step?

- You erred on the side of communication and clarification?
- You took one less thing for granted?
- You got a better night's sleep?
- You could learn to be content regardless of external factors?
- You disrupted a social norm?
- You smiled more often?
- You experimented more?
- You already beat lottery-winning odds just by being alive?
- Opportunities abound, and it's just a matter of tuning in to them?
- You don't have to do anything to prove your inherent worth?
- Here is just as good as there?
- This is as ready as you'll ever be?
- The person you are envious of isn't actually all that happy?
- All is forgiven?
- The worst actually happens?
- You can still become passionately interested in something new?
- You matter?
- There is life after heartbreak?
- That fortune cookie was right that said: "Nature, time, and patience are the three great physicians"?
- The experts are wrong?
- There's hope?
- This is all just a dream?
- 2021 will be as good as you decide to make it, come what may?

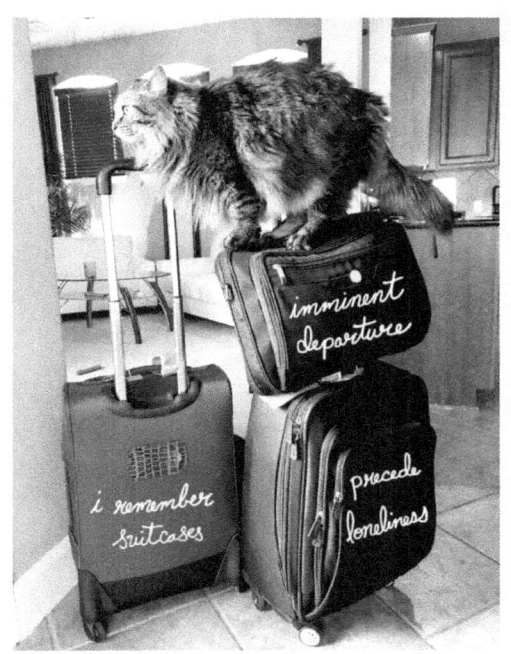

Departure by Matt & Madelinne

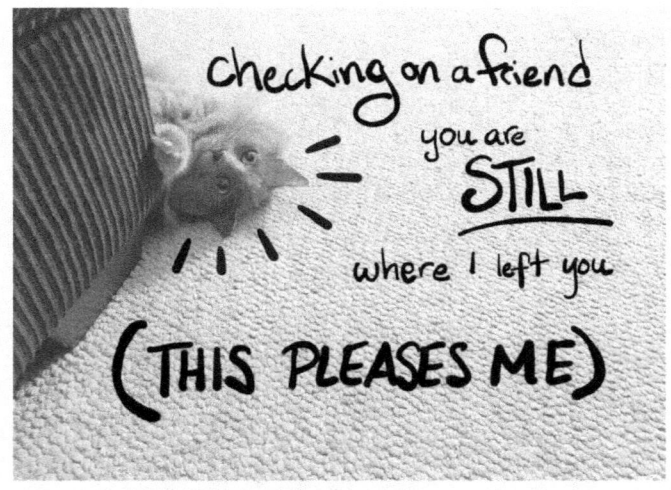

Friend by Matt & Madelinne

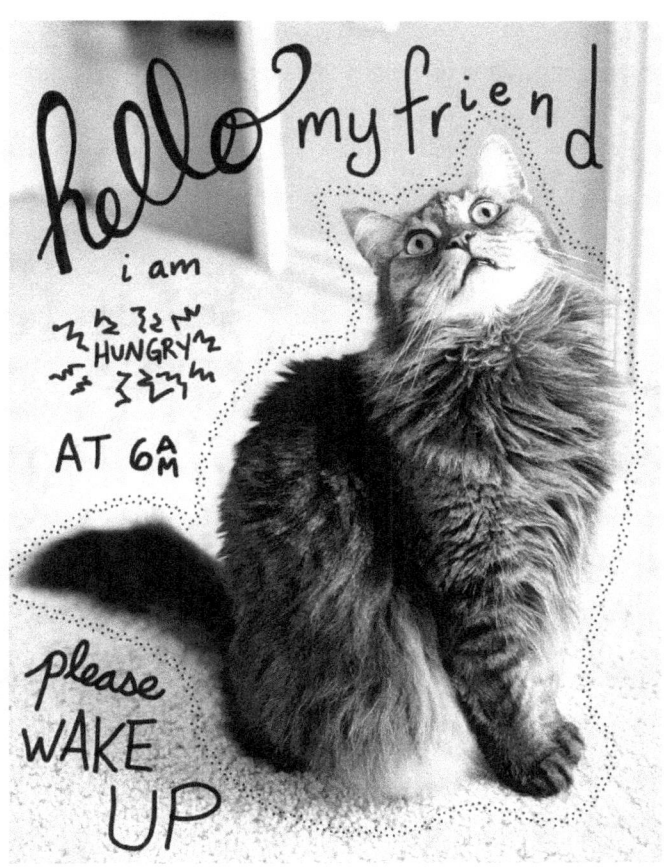

Hungry by Matt & Madelinne

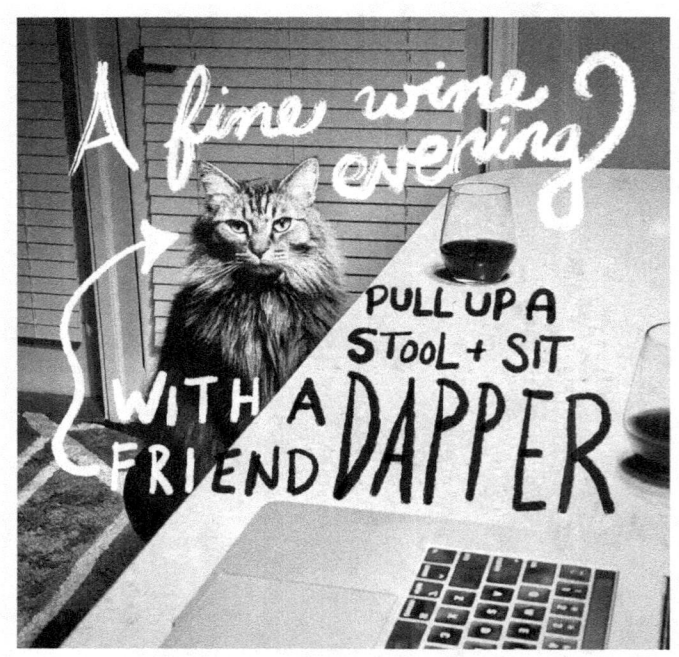

Dapper by Matt & Madelinne

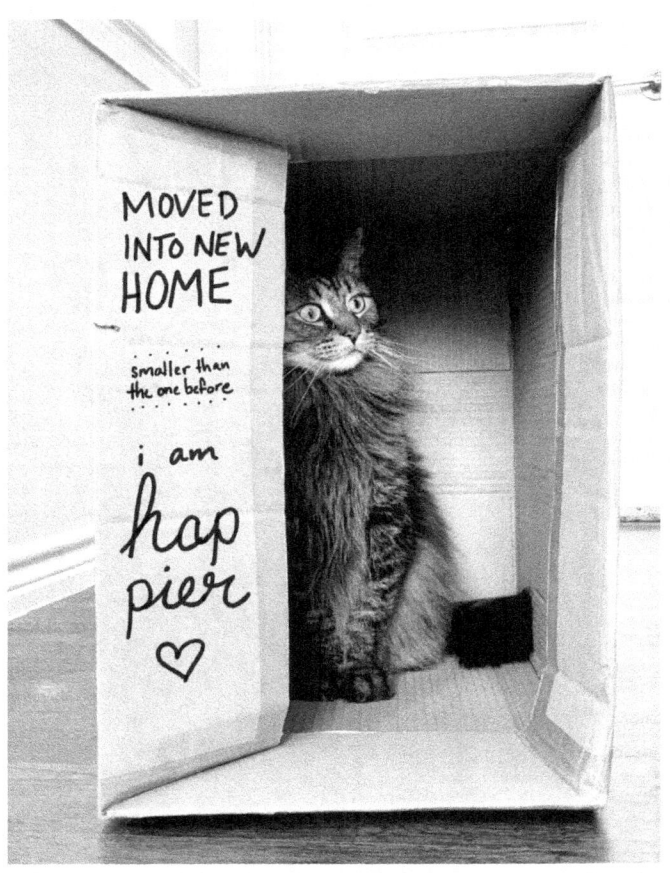

Home by Matt & Madelinne

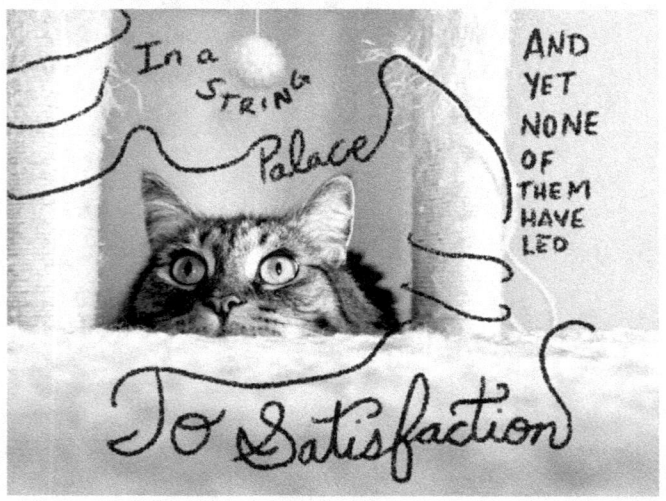

String by Matt & Madelinne

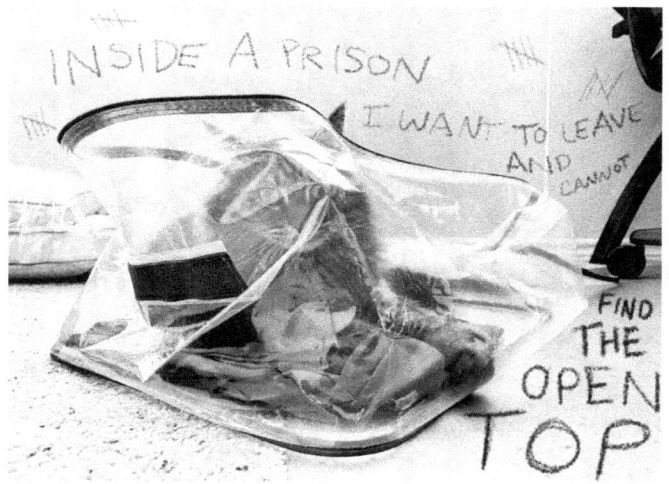

Prison by Matt & Madelinne

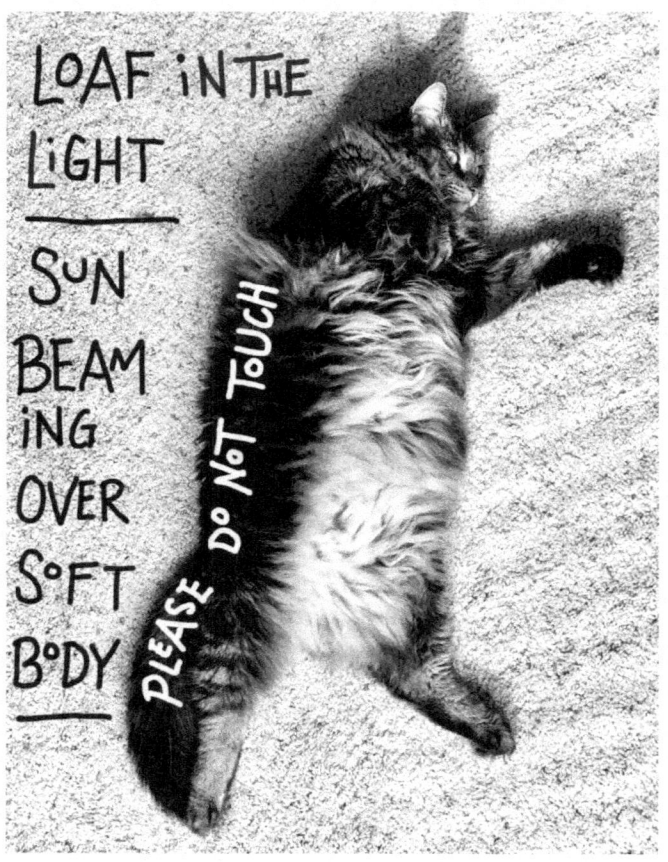

Loaf by Matt & Madelinne

I'VE SPENT days thinking about what I'd like to contribute to this book. I decided, finally, that I'd like to use this as an opportunity to open up, be vulnerable, and share some of the hard times and sweet breakthroughs I've achieved this year. Like other human beings, I fear judgement, criticism, and ostracism. While I worry that what I share here might leave some people shocked, I know this group well enough to believe that they will love and accept me no matter what. And it certainly helps that I'm writing this under a pseudonym and none outside my trusted sphere of friends would recognise me.

For a long time, I've struggled to manage my deep anxiety, bottled up emotions, and what at one point seemed like pervasive depression. Depression runs rampant in my father's side of the family so it wasn't surprising to me that I was showing the signs too. Added to it was the fact that I came from a pretty orthodox Hindu Brahmin family with strict rules to follow which added to my feelings of suppression. During my teen years and early twenties, I stumbled upon a way to 'handle' my issues. I found that inflicting self-harm was perfect because I could do it in secret by myself, didn't need to seek external help, and couldn't be told off or judged for it (as long as no one got the wind of it). It wasn't pretty, it wasn't safe, but it was effective, so I embraced it quietly and quickly. I never took to cutting (I hate the sight of blood) or burning (I was too scared to do that) but I did hit myself (usually with my own hands but sometimes with other objects), bang my head, scratch myself, dig my fingernails deeply into my skin, especially under another fingernail (sometimes to the extent that the latter would start bleeding). I hurt myself until the physical pain overrode any and all other emotions I was feeling and the voices in my head stopped. Then I'd breathe freely once again and my rational mind would return. The relief I felt during those few moments would be followed up with horror at what I'd done, shame, and regret. Sometimes these feelings would last for days, eroding my self-esteem and I'd resolve to 'never, ever do it again'. So why did I keep going back to viciously hitting and scratching myself? My theory is that I knew that I didn't feel suicidal or want to inflict any *serious* harm upon myself. I wanted to cause myself just enough pain to feel in control of my anxiety and emotions. And since that was the best available tool, I didn't want to give it up.

As the years passed, the number of 'episodes', as I called them, became fewer and fewer. When I was doing particularly well emotionally and mentally, I didn't even consider self-harm. Strangely enough, I found that when I started working in sales, these episodes became a rarity. During intensely trying times in my relationships, though, these became frequent.

In March this year, thanks to Covid, I moved out of my own place and in with my family after eight years of being away from home. Now, don't mistake me, I love my family. My grandparents are the most understanding, loving, caring, respectful, and non-interfering people so it's quite easy to get along with them. My mother is a sweetheart with a sunshiny spirit and a kind heart. It's fun and easy to be around her too. So it wasn't like I was moving into a hostile environment; quite the contrary.

Maybe it was the challenge of adjusting to the new life-style or the general state that the Covid lockdown thrust upon us, but I started feeling stressed, anxious, and stifled in my new home by May. The orthodox religious rules I was expected to follow were beginning to weigh me down. One fine day it all became too much, I had a major 'episode' which sent me into a state of panic. After it happened, I locked myself in a room and cried for hours before I felt calm enough to reemerge. My mind was reeling. Where had that *come* from? I felt deeply ashamed because I'd lost control in front of my mother. She's an understanding, compassionate and non-judgmental woman but I still felt terrible. It became apparent to me that I needed help. I'd worked with therapists before and knew the benefits of having one. But when I reached out to the therapist I'd worked with before, I found out that she was unavailable. That sent me into further panic. This was the person I'd worked with since 2017! How was I going to find a new person I'd feel comfortable enough to open up to?

Almost on a whim and maybe because I desperately needed an outlet to calm myself, I decided to share this incident with a new friend I'd made that month. I mostly expected that he would be supportive, but a part of me was fearful that he'd want nothing to do with me once he heard about this side to me. I needn't have worried, though. The sort of understanding, compassion, and support he expressed sent tears rolling down my cheeks. "The next time you feel the need to vent, use me as a punchbag. Send 50 texts if you need to. Do whatever it takes to feel better. I'm here for you", he said. That helped me calm down considerably.

I kept my hunt for a good therapist on even as I read as much as I could online about my abnormal and scary behaviour. After getting in touch with about a dozen therapists, I got referred to my current therapist, Natasha, by my financial advisor. I think I gave her a call within a couple hours of getting hold of her number. "I have a problem", I said and launched into an explanation of why I needed a therapist and now. By the end of it, I was self-diagnosing and spouting a bunch of conditions from BPD to ADHD. She listened intently until I finished and said mildly, "You know, I prefer not to label any person. That's not to say you aren't experiencing what you are and they should certainly be addressed. It might be better to do that without the burden of labels, that's all. Why don't we set up a call for Thursday? We can talk in a bit more detail."

I went into that first session desperate to know what was wrong with me. I was determined to uncover my deepest, darkest issues once and for all! I felt that all my issues since childhood would finally be brought to light and a path to solving them paved. Instead, Natasha requested that I give her a background about me. Maybe it was the awareness that I was speaking to a stranger, but I stuck to the professional stuff. When I got to the point of talking about leaving my startup, unexpectedly, I broke down. What the hell? I thought I'd long since gotten over the pain of leaving the company I'd started from scratch...but apparently not. The wounds hadn't healed fully yet, clearly.

Maybe that was the first insight I had in therapy. Just

because time had passed didn't mean that I was done grieving or that a wound had healed. Sometimes the pattern, grief, or experience runs deep and it takes a while to process and release it. I also noticed that there was a flip side to this. Some wounds, even traumatic ones, were truly healed and didn't bring up any difficult emotions in me. For example, when I talked about my sexual assault in 2017, I was quite calm. That was in stark contrast to the subject of leaving my startup which had brought on uncontrolled sobbing which, by all external markers, would seem like less of a catastrophe. We humans are strange.

As the weeks passed, I realised that the tendency to inflict self-harm wasn't one single giant blob of an issue; rather, it was a mosaic of multiple issues. I was beginning to see the rationale behind not labelling this tendency and working on isolated issues that could help me have a better sense of control and handle situations better. Some 'issues' seemed laughably simple and fixable while others felt insurmountable:

Feeling like I didn't have enough physical space or privacy. Feeling like my boundaries were being violated often. Feeling like I was cornered. Feeling like I couldn't speak up and was bottling up emotions. Feeling like no one wanted a part in my healing process and would hate me for my issues. Feeling lonely. Feeling undeserving of love.

It was quite mind-boggling to notice the torrent of under-lying beliefs, experiences, and expectations that made up my psyche and dictated my actions. Was I really that compli-cated, I wondered. But just discussing experiences, though not always easy, helped me process them and get a deeper understanding of myself. It's helped me see that my reactions were not altogether out of the ordinary. A large part of it was a very *human* reaction though not always rational or the best.

The slow understanding and embracing of myself as a human being and not the perfect person I so wished I were helped bridge my expectations of who I wanted to be and the reality of who I was. That has been immensely freeing. To hold space for myself with my flaws and all is the best gift I've given myself this year.

While most sessions were ordinary, some of them were truly extraordinary and I achieved what I felt were true breakthroughs. I'll share the details of one particular session with you. We were discussing the topic of jealousy; something I've battled for a long time in various contexts - with family, romantic partners, friends, classmates, coworkers. Whenever I experience jealousy, it is accompanied by shame, guilt, and frustration because I don't *want* to feel that way.

Somehow, the discussion breadcrumbs led us to exploring an incident when I was six years old. It was playtime in school and all the kids were running toward the playground, excited to be running away from the classroom toward an hour of freedom and joy. I was running too. I'm not sure how it happened, but I remember seeing the girl running in front of me go sprawling on the hard ground and beginning to cry loudly. I was horror struck even as I apologised for what I'd done, helped her stand up, and brushed the dust off her uniform. And then came the thumps on my back, shoulders, and arms. I fell to the ground, bewildered and scared as the bunch of kids standing around me in a circle continued to hit me. I remember crying and landing a few whacks of my own on them. I also remember running to the teacher at one point and imploring her to help me only to receive a vague smile and no intervention. The shock, pain, fear, and anger I felt that day never really left me. What's more, six year-old me interpreted that whole incident to mean that I was, at a fundamental level, unloveable and that I'd always be shunned by others.

I was crying as I narrated the incident to my therapist; the pain was real. It was kinda weird to think that that one incident that had happened 24 years ago was still something that impacted me in a deep way today. My therapist asked me to close my eyes and visualise myself back in the playground as the present-day me, watching the scene unfold all the while feeling all the emotions the 6-year-old me was feeling. After I'd watched the whole thing from a distance, she asked me to walk over to my six-year-old self and give her a hug. She asked me to take a minute and think about what message I'd like her to hear. I came up with three:

"Everything will turn out okay"

"You are loved"

"You are brave"

That visualisation/dialogue was one of the most powerfully cathartic things I've ever experienced. It gave me a deeper understanding of where my (erroneous) belief of not being loved or accepted by others came from. My jealousy was often triggered because deep down, since I believed that I wasn't loveable, I felt that I couldn't ever have that which others had - love and acceptance. Another interesting thing is how the human mind uses cues from experiences to reinforce beliefs. So whenever I felt that I had behaved badly or done something unpleasant, my brain whispered, "See? *That's* why you're not loveable!" Years and years of this pattern repeated...I can only imagine the number I must've played on myself.

Getting a fundamental understanding where my beliefs stem from, why I act the way I do, and how my experiences have shaped me has made it so much easier for me to be more accepting and compassionate toward myself. It's helped me believe that change is possible and that I'm indeed capable of growth. Over the course of the last several months, I've grown and changed so much. What's been even more amazing to watch is how feeling positively toward myself has flown outward and helped me feel positively toward others. I see everyone else as a fellow passenger, dealing with their own problems and being on their own growth journeys. I feel a sense of camaraderie and am a bit more relaxed while sharing my own trials and tribulations. I find it easier to listen with a more empathetic and non-judgmental ear to other people's struggles.

I'd like to think that I've become better at showing forbearance, compassion, and gratitude. Things that might have disgusted or troubled me in the past, at least in many cases, no longer do because the lens with which I view them has changed. The other day, I saw that my grandfather had soiled himself. To my surprise, I felt extremely compassionate toward him which probably wouldn't have been my first reaction even a couple of years ago. As we got him cleaned up, I thought about how as you become old, you become a child again; helpless, innocent, and dependent on others to take care of you. If I'm lucky, I'll one day get to be 89 years old too. And I sure as hell hope that my mother gets to live to be 89 and I'll have the chance to take care of her. I thought about the time when my paternal grandfather died of colon cancer in early 2017 after suffering from it for a six months. My startup was young at the time and I was working relentlessly to get it off the ground. Before I knew it, he had passed away and I still grieve the fact that I didn't spend enough time with him during his last days. Looking at my maternal grandfather, I suddenly felt overwhelming gratitude for this year and all the time I had got to spend with my family.

While I'm glad that I've changed for the better, what's

truly been satisfying is the process of becoming itself. The realisation that I'm a work in progress and always will be allows me to enjoy the process and not feel dejected by my flaws or mistakes. This has also helped me stay compassionate and patient towards myself. This year, I've perhaps had four episodes of self-harm, with the most intense one being the one in May. The more understanding I've had of myself, the way my brain works, and the past patterns that are at play, the better I've become at reassuring myself and having faith that I am and will be okay, no matter what. Sometimes it feels like there's barely any progress and I'm back to where I was 10 years ago. But that's never true. I'm never regressing, I'm always progressing. So long as I'm continually working toward being a better version of myself, there's bound to be progress.

I am more aware than ever of all the things I still struggle with and want to change about myself. I'd like to become better at taking up space and letting others help and support me. I'd like to get way better at communicating my needs and wants and establishing boundaries. I'd like to truly accept that I'm deserving of love. I'd like to trust that people accept me for who I am and I don't need to be anyone other than who I am. I'd like to be a lot less insecure and jealous. I'm also still very, very aware of my self-harming tendencies and that it will probably take a lot more time and effort to wean myself off of those long-established patterns. The difference now, after several months of therapy, self-exploration, and loving social support is that it's a *hopeful* awareness. As 2020 year draws to a close, I feel gratitude for having access to an extraordinary therapist, for the transformation I've experienced, and for the truly amazing people I have in my life.

And I can't wait to see what 2021 has in store for me.

CHAPTER 9
HEALING CREATIVE SCARS WITH
DOODLING

BY CC

ONE OF MY earliest creative memories is at the age of six. I started school one year early, so have always had classmates a year older than me.

I remember sitting at my desk in school, happily drawing a house in a park. The biggest part of the drawing was the sky, and I was determined to finish it. I sat there for a long time, coloring it with blue crayons. It was all over the place, but I had so much fun doing it.

While absorbed in the task, a boy in my class came up beside me: "Are you six years old?" he asked. "Yes?", I replied. He glanced down at my work: "I can tell by the way you draw."

A small, probably not malicious, but a not-so-nice comment, that could have easily passed me by. But boy did it leave a mark. I already had insecurities about being the youngest in the class. This comment confirmed part of my suspicions that I was inferior; at least creatively.

I haven't thought about this incident that often, but for sure I've internalized this belief into my identity of not being artistic. "Oh, I just can't draw," and "No, I don't do 'art'.

Music is my thing." A running joke has been that I can't even draw a stick figure.

Brené Brown talks about this in her 2015 book, *Daring Greatly*. She writes about how 85% of the people she interviewed in her shame research had a childhood memory that was shaming enough to change how they perceived themselves as learners. Half of these experiences, in turn, she referred to as having made 'creative scars'.

Expressing ourselves creatively is a vulnerable act. So when we're questioned or maybe laughed at, it can hurt on a deeper level. Whether conscious or not, it can shape how we perceive ourselves and the choices we make based on it.

It's like sharing a secret with someone. If you're met with judgment or ridicule, the trust and connection you're seeking is squashed. If your secret gets space and empathy, it can grow into something different.

I've been thinking a lot about creativity over the last few months. I was hoping for a year of outer expansion and **more**. More travel, more business, more love and more social connections. 2020 has panned out very differently for all of us, and I can see how the expansion I was looking to create instead has grown on the inside.

One piece of this puzzle? A month ago, I signed up for a "doodle" course with a friend, where we're learning beginner-level visual elements; drawing faces, stick figures, objects etc. Everyday I've been learning new shapes, and slowly but steadily my stick figure is coming alive. He's now walking, sitting, jumping, meditating and swimming.

And I've been able to share it with a group of people who cheer me on. "Hi guys, here's my doodle. What do you think?" The first few shares, it was not the adult me showing my doodles. It was more like a six-year old girl who wanted someone to say that my creativity didn't suck. "Is this OK?" "Am *I* OK?"

I love the metaphor of fire. As I share more, that tiny flicker of expression has grown into a flame. Maybe someday it will be a fire. It no longer matters as much what others say about my drawing, it's about my own experience with doodling and my own relationship to art.

So I'm feeding the flame of creativity and joy, wondering how to grow it into a fire. This process has made me wonder what other potential flames I've squashed in my life.

What flickers, flames or fires do you want to nurture?

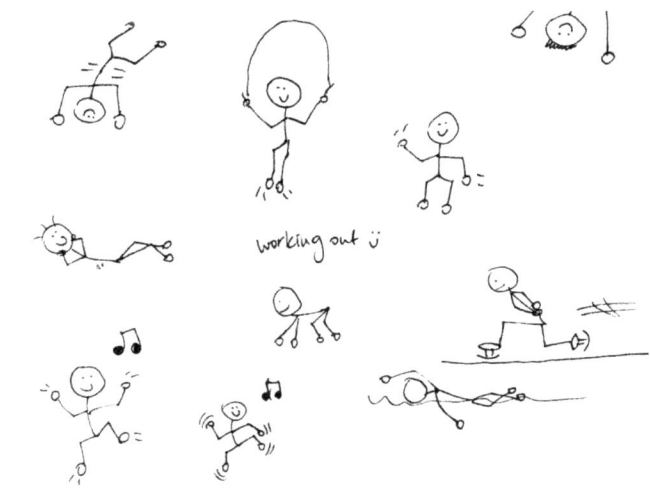

Stick figures from Day 12 of the Doodle course :)

CHAPTER 10
WEAKDAYS

BY AZMAT

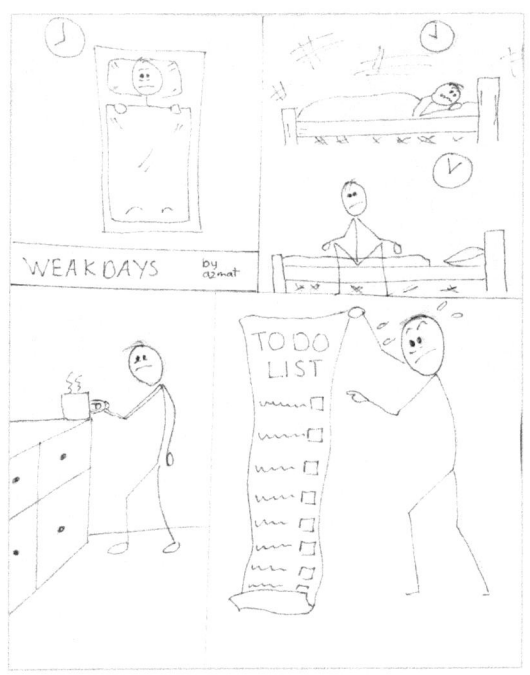

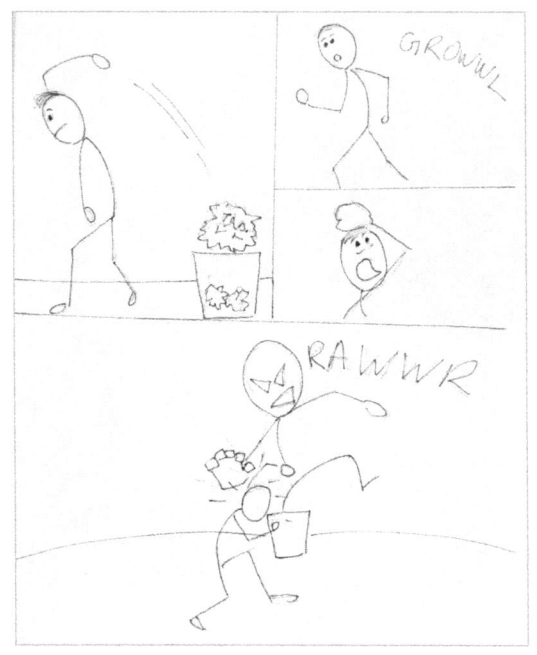

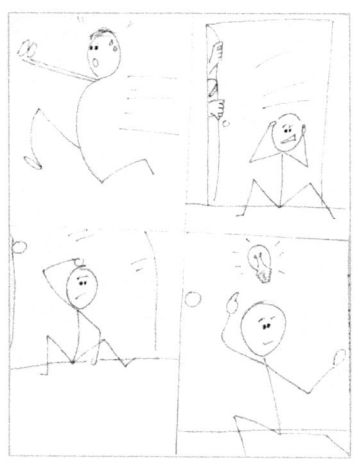

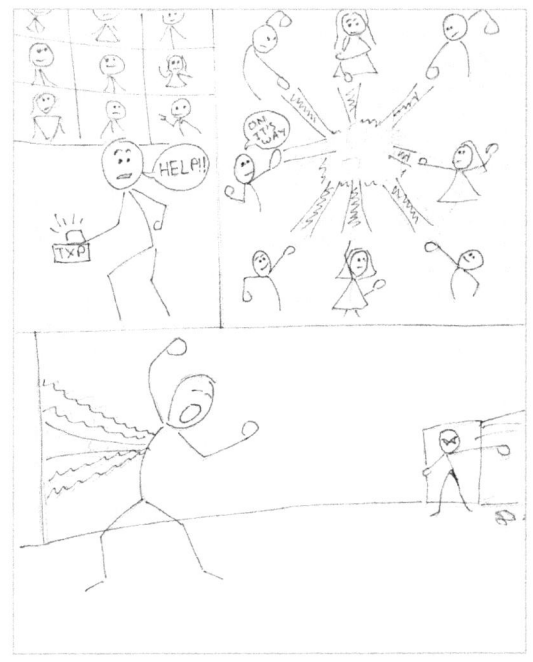

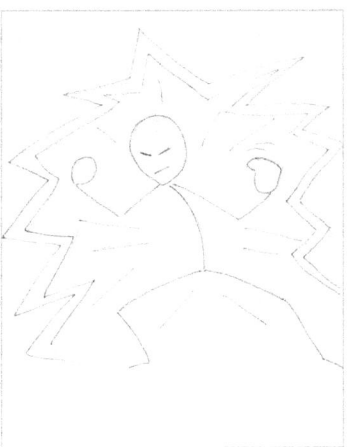

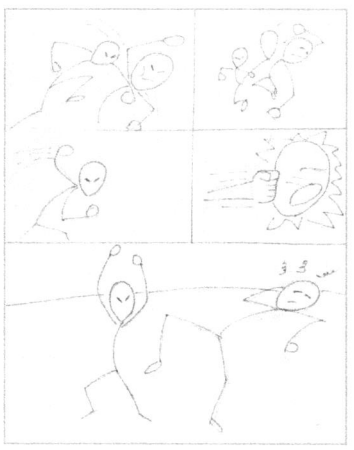

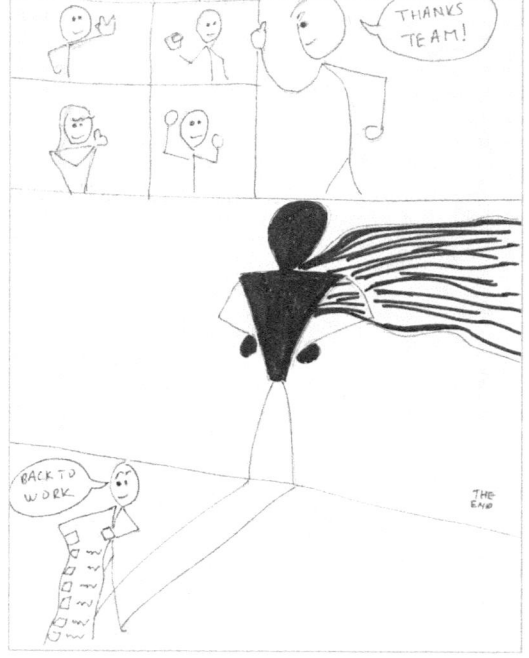

PERSEPHONE

I WAS HAPPY.

Happy in the way where you don't think about it too much, in the way you are pragmatic, in the way you say to life, "You have given me the playbook, and I will follow the rules". Before, when I was younger, I didn't follow the rules, and I wasn't happy. I quit high school, I didn't go to college, and earned only the bare minimum amount of money to survive. I wrote music and played loud rock shows and lived in my art and my vices. I had a repertoire of unsatisfactory boyfriends, trying to grasp the elusive rainbow of satisfaction, always just out of reach.

Perhaps pragmatism happens in your late twenties as a default setting, an alarm clock that's been snoozed too long. Perhaps the painful experiences I endured when I was younger spooked me straight. Regardless, I started following the rules, the ones that tell you to get married, have a child, buy a house, settle down, be an adult. And I was happy, and I thought maybe I was even satisfied. It looked that way, and I thought the way it looked was the way it was.

Within the borders of my new life, I wrote songs (but not too many), I laughed (but not quite so loudly), and excavated gratitude (who could say I wasn't lucky?).

When I write lyrics, they come from somewhere further inside of myself than I can see. I seldom grasp them in the moment, but trust their truth, which is revealed to me over the passage of time. *Persephone* was one such song, an orbiting song for the new album I would go on to create, an album I couldn't have dreamed of creating at the time, in the simple trappings of my conventional life.

Now that I'm all better.
Now that I'm not who I used to be.
Now that I'm a little older.
I can wake up from nightmares.
Now that I've started over
I know endings aren't beautiful, they're messy.
Now that I've sailed along the Acheron
I can live through a nightmare.
I'm in the calm blue water.
This is not the life of my dreams.
One foot in the underworld like Persephone
But the sun is shining on me.
Maybe my edges are softer
The waves have polished these rocks
Oh I guess that makes me a fire.
I wanted to be, I wanted to be.
I wanted to be.
I want it to be.

ONE MORE DAY

You can paint the past any which way you want. I could write that I was happy, and maybe that could be true. I could write that I was unhappy, and there would be plenty of supporting evidence for that too. It's the picture I want to create, the story I want to tell, and that's what's true.

I wasn't happy, if happiness means depth and richness and feeling free and unlimited, feeling like the god of my reality. I was unhappy, if unhappiness means being small and contained, the smiling housewife to the god of my reality.

Combing through my journals, all the way back to 2012 when I first met my husband-to-be, the pieces were there. The familiar restlessness, the wanting more. But at the time, I told a different story, and I believed it too.

I wrote One More Day in 2013 when I lived in Texas, lonely without him. "Why can't you just quit your job, drop everything and come live in Texas with me?" I asked him so many times, in so many different words. An unreasonable request – "change your life for me". An unreasonable request – "love me so much that you shed your pragmatism".

He visited me once, but of course he didn't drop everything. Life went on like normal.

One more day, then I'll think about jumping in with you.
One more day of this, toes in the swimming pool.
Oh look where'd the time go, suddenly older.
Time spent watching and now the water's cold.
It eats me up inside.
One more day, what if I can't afford to
Give up all I've got just to be close to you?
Can't you see these clothes on my back are dry?
And it's getting late, I think I'll just go back inside.

It eats me up inside.
One more day, waiting for the sun to rise.
And all of these days flash before my eyes.
Every snapshot, lens focused on wanting.
Hoping just turned into haunting.
It eats me up inside.

PRECIPICE

But why be small? Why be afraid? It was 2019, and I was finally doing well with my business – well enough that I could afford a little cubicle of an office space – and I finally had access to childcare (though only three days a week and an hour's drive from my home). In the quietude of my cubicle, after I had finished the requisite piano lessons, I'd find myself writing. Something that had been closed inside of me for years had opened a crack, and a trickle of inspiration came through. The inspiration came from myself, but it also came from him. He found the light switch, the door, the well, some other metaphor. With the light on, with the trickle through the open door, with water to drink, I started to rediscover myself, one word at a time.

We talked about many things that autumn. One such thing was reminiscing about our dead selves. In that cubicle, I felt like I was seventeen again, as though way back then I'd hit the pause button on that version of myself, scrolled through other characters in my twenties, and resumed the character I used to be as I entered age thirty-three, the character who really *felt* the life she lived, who wasn't yet too scared.

The story you write is the story you experience, so if I tell you I felt, at that moment in time, like I was about to step off a cliff into the unknown, then I'm also admitting that I created that feeling. But I wrote *Precipice* as a song of hope, a mantra of courage, before I'd decided to end my marriage but not long before. I wanted to believe that I'd be okay if I jumped from my safe life, that I could survive any pain, that no matter what happened to me, I'd always be okay.

"I'm worried about you," Rob wrote me when I shared the demo with him. "This is really fucking depressing."

"It's not depressing," I told him. "I say 'I will be okay.'"

"Yeah," he replied. "Lost alone in the dark."

But it's easy to be okay in the light, with others, and with a map. That doesn't take any courage at all.

Can I be okay, barefoot in the dark,
Lost without a light, save for the one inside?
Can I move on, no matter how far?
Lay my dead selves to rest,
And the one that's left,
Let her heart open wide.
Let my heart open wide.
Can I trust the sense of my heart?
That there's nothing I need,
And there's nothing to lose?
Can I find peace in falling apart?
Stumbling in the night,
Blending black and white,
My edges diffused.
My edges diffused.
Can I melt into the question,
My body into air,
No in here or out there?
But still keep my sure footing,
One step, then another,
Even if I never know where
It is

I'm going
I will be okay, lost alone in the dark.
I will be okay, lost alone in the dark.
I will be okay, lost alone in the dark.

Note: Later, I would insist to Rob that this be the last song on the album. How the critical moment of the album's journey was deciding to step off the cliff. He wanted to cut the song completely; we'd been struggling to create something out of it, to get it just right. *Precipice* was his problem song. (*Hostage* was mine, as I'll share later.) My hope, secret except to all of you, is that this one ends up being his proudest work on the album.

DEAR DISASTER

It was 2012, the year of *The Avengers*, Obama's re-election, and Instagram's arrival on Android devices. Michael and I dove head-first into a serious relationship, saying "fuck it" to the unspoken rule of not dating your bandmate. It was the year we recorded our first album. It was the year our band broke up.

We were jamming in the large upstairs music studio where I worked, our custom on Sunday afternoons. The four of us were practicing a new song that we had played live once or twice, but we hadn't quite worked out the ending improvisation section.

Rob was there, and who knows why. Rob shows up in my life during tumultuous moments, on cue, and I convene in his life in the same manner. So it happened that he was there when our guitarist said he was done. It was the summertime and our album was scheduled to be released in September.

Our bassist said that he should probably opt out too; he had three kids, after all.

I didn't say anything. I walked out of the studio, down the stairs and into the break room, putting my head in my hands. Michael was close behind, my partner in getting dumped. Rob sat with us.

How perfect, I thought, that the last song The Criminal Kid worked on together was about breaking up, about a compulsion toward destruction, a love of starting over and rebuilding. The lyrics are brief, weaving with the most beautiful part our guitarist had ever written, simple and plain, interspersed by meandering piano notes.

(*Note: He recorded this guitar part, and this guitar part only, for the new album.*) The second half of the song would come to be instrumental, all chaos and percussion and crashing. *Dear Disaster* became the song of my band's end, and later, the song of my marriage's end.

I want to tear the tower down,
Get reacquainted with the ground.
On the edge of a beautiful view,
Where's it going to lead you?
What's right is always close inside,
That little voice that cannot lie.
The truth won't sleep, it'll haunt your dreams.
When you know, you gotta let go.

BLACK WATER

My worst month of 2020 was January. It was certainly worse for other people in later months because of the pandemic. The pandemic brought struggles to my life just like everyone else, but January was the crash after the rush of cliff-jumping.

I was alone. My marriage was over. Everything was new, and nothing was stable. I was slowly working up the courage to tell my family about my Great Failure, because a failed marriage is one of the Great Failures of life. Alongside going bankrupt or going to prison.

He was there sometimes, but my comrade in ending a relationship was dealing with his own crash, and he didn't have the capacity to build something with me. Plus, he was far away and across a border. I was alone and the world was cold and dark and I kept it together because my daughter was alongside me for most of it.

One evening, sprawled on the living room rug, staring up at the ceiling, I felt the familiar tug to write. It's usually a gentle tug, easy to ignore, and I've ignored it too many times. *Not now, muse. I'm busy.* But this time, I felt the tug and I took to my notebook like there was no other choice, because I suppose there wasn't.

The words came out quickly. I sang whisper-quiet at the piano since my daughter was sleeping upstairs. *Black Water* was the fastest-written song on the album. Some songs take years (*Natural Feelings* was originally incepted in 2004, with further development in 2015), and some songs take hours. The quality seems to suffer more with the longer-written songs, since these need to be carefully excavated like dinosaur bones. The fast ideas are the ones you get to pull from loose sand without resistance. These songs feel like a gift from the Muse.

Even in the hardest moments, though, I knew I was strong enough to grit my teeth and get through the pain. I'd done it before, and I will surely do it again. Rob might say it's another depressing song, another one to give him anxiety about my mental state, but it's not just a song of rock-bottom. It's a song of survival. The moon never sinks in the water, after all. It just seems that way.

Loosen the string
I'm too strong to let it go.
Feel the sting
Burning hands grasp this rope.
I'm too proud to let you know.
Up in the atmosphere
Get carried away
But I'm too sure to float
I'll steer it this way.
Always headed for hope
I'm too far to let it go.
And I don't know if you'll find me here
But I'll go there anyway.
I'm too lost in the smoke
Too bright in the black
So I'll swim in the gray sky
Swim in the gray sky
Moving the tides just to
Try to move you.
It's dark again, the sun will rise
But I don't know when.
Right now I just need a friend.
I'm too lost in the smoke
Too bright in the dark
I'll sink in the black water
Extinguish in the water.
Past the horizon line
A part of the tides.
Just to find something new.
It's dark again, the sun will rise

But I don't know when.
Right now I just need an end.

ALL YOUR WORDS

I don't think it's so unusual for the worst years to be the best years, because they're the years you're really alive. And that's the prize, isn't it?

I wish I could remember what you said
I wish I could remember what you said
And hear all the ways that you said it
And hear all the ways that you said it to me.
I want to remember all the words,
I want to remember it all.
I want to remember all the words,
I want to remember it all.
I wish I could recall your body language
I wish I could recall your body language
And see all the ways that you moved
And see all the ways that you moved with me.
I want to remember all the words,
I want to remember it all.
I want to remember all the words,
I want to remember it all.

SHIVER IN THE SUN

Albums fall together in their own time. The universe handles the details, and I try to get out of the way and remember my place as a conduit.

I knew the album was to be a collection of songs about relationships – of endings and beginnings – and I knew that I wanted it to be called *Conversations with You in My Head*. Like Modest Mouse, I have a penchant for long album titles (though if I'm to make a third album, it'll be just one word). I liked the title as a symbol of fear. Of not having the conversations you really want – or need – to have, of having a fear of manifesting yourself and your deepest desires.

This album is a journey from inner to outer. From the conversations I'd have in my head, to actual conversations. No longer just thoughts, but realities, and later memories, with all their consequences. That was my journey this year, *courage,* the word I'd chosen for 2020, and I needed that word desperately. The album was to be about ownership, where the thing to be owned is yourself. *The god of your reality.* No more playing someone else's game.

Shiver in the Sun was the track I worried about the most. Every song on the album started as a vocal and piano solo, but some songs are better suited to that than others. *Persephone* and *Black Water* work that way. But *Shiver* was destined to be a driving rock song, and it was difficult to imagine what it would become from the sloppy demo I shared with Rob, Michael and our recording engineer.

The vocals are challenging; fast and nimble, and in the low-to-mid range, the hardest range to control, when a controlled sound is crucial to the message. The piano is challenging too; both hands in constant motion, at 160 beats per minute, and a solo in the latter half.

Shiver tells the story of the album, where the "sun" could be any variety of things – life, of course, and death, but also romantic love, and also a dream. And all those things all at once.

Shiver in the sun 'cause there's no other
I wanted to know, I wanted to know

Where will I go?
I could waste away so slowly you wouldn't see
I wanted to know, I wanted to know
Where would I go?
This high velocity curiosity
I wanted to know, I wanted to know
What if I let go?
I wanted to know, I wanted to know,
What if I let go?
Is there nothing left of these promises?
I swore to you I'd never give in.
But dreams are so much easier to live in.
Clouds creating shadows in my moods
I wanted to know, I wanted to know,
Where do we go?
If nothing ever gets where it's going to
I wanted to know, I wanted to know
Why I can't move slow.
This high velocity curiosity
I already know, I already know,
No I can't move slow.
I already know, I already know,
No I can't move slow.
Is there nothing left of these promises?
I swore to you I'd never give in.
But dreams are so much easier to live in.
Permanence is permeating silence
I wanted to know, I wanted to know
Where will we go?
The best I ever had was free and giving
I wanted to know, I wanted to know
If I could call it my own.
I wanted to know, I wanted to know,

If I could call you my own.
Shiver in the sun
Shiver in the sun
Shiver in the sun

WHAT ARE YOU WAITING FOR

Some of the songs on this album originate from over a decade ago; I am meticulous in saving my ideas, even the really bad ones. Most of my ideas are bad, maybe even 9/10ths of them. Some of these ideas die, and remain dead, unresurrectable. But some are just sleeping, cryogenic, and can be defrosted by The Muse.

Other songs are new, and very much Of the Moment. My songwriting frenzy in the first half of 2020 finished with *What Are You Waiting For*, written just prior to going into the studio. I seldom write Of the Moment lyrics, preferring to write retrospectively, long after I've caught my breath from my inner rollercoasters. Few songs end up being a snapshot of time (*Black Water* is another such rare one). Most of my songs are outside of time, and I like it that way.

But *What Are You Waiting For* was a song I wrote one weekend in May to communicate with him beyond conversation. I thought lyrics set to music would have more impact, but truthfully, I was also afraid to have those conversations with him, so I hid behind my lyrics.

Somehow the song formed in a different way than anything I'd ever written. Even the original naked piano demo was syncopated and sexy, a style I had never explored. I wrote a line in the lyric that Rob would later ask about —

"Did you mean to imply this? It makes me blush to read."

It's not my best song or my best lyric, but it's playful and serious at the same time, which feels very much like *me*. It is the least cryptic song on the album, and I hardly need to assist in interpretation, except to mention that the specific events and circumstances that led to the writing of this were real in a way that my music seldom is. But even still, this song is just a costume, just a character, just a story being told.

Come on move on in my direction
Get your feet on the ground, get your feet on the ground.
Close the distance, all the pain's in the waiting,
Tell me what miracle are you waiting for?
Come on I think I know what you want
Come on just stop looking at the ashes,
It's just a reaction.
Oh love I think you know what you want,
Oh love just stop looking for disaster,
It's just a distraction.
I want you to be so deep into me that you can't sleep.
I want to be what you need, maybe then I'll feel complete.
I want a love that hurts so deep that it sets me free.
I want to be what you need, let this fire consume me.
So serious, everything means everything
Gets to be all too much, it's all too much.
Lighten up, it's all so important and it crowns you with a
crutch,
It's all too much.
Come on I think I know what you want
Come on just stop looking over the edge,
And jump in.
Oh love I think you know what you want
But you'll never know until you're all in,
So just jump in.
Just a minute, just a minute, wait just a minute.
Just a minute, wait just a minute, wait just a minute.

I want you to be so deep into me that you can't sleep.
I want to be what you need, maybe then I'll feel complete.
I want a love that hurts so deep that it sets me free.
I want to be what you need, let this fire consume me.

NATURAL FEELINGS

It's hard not to look at my teenage self with rose-tinted glasses. Back then, I had as much fire as I've ever had, but I couldn't control it. I would burn and destroy and blind, myself most of all. I would stay up until sunrise and sleep all day and fill journals with untethered thoughts and get stoned with my band and listen to albums in a way that moved my heart, a heart that grew stonier and unaffected with time. My dreams were big because I hadn't yet been disappointed, and I was unafraid because I hadn't yet been truly scared, and I was very happy because I was still a kid, and I was very sad because I didn't know what real sadness was, and I was very lonely because I didn't know who I was, but there was still so much *magic* back then, back before everything could be understood or explained. A thing you can explain becomes an ordinary thing, and thus I became an ordinary thing. But that was just a stop along the way; the next stop on my journey of understanding was humility. Maybe I wasn't knowable, maybe I didn't have it all figured out. A return to the blank slate of youth, but with the information of adulthood. Manufactured magic. You're the god, you create it.

I returned to that self nearly two decades later, laying my other dead selves to rest, *time in between was just a dream* . What a trip to be seventeen-times-two. What a trip to feel like that again; the highs, the lows, the magic, the fire, the story, *the fucking story*. Being able to control the fire (maybe, probably, hopefully) after another lifetime spinning with the world.

I wrote the first line of *Natural Feelings* on a scrap of paper in a bathroom when I was eighteen. We had done blades that night, and I was detached from anything ordinary, and my mind had been blown by live recordings of the White Stripes, and I was elated from partying with the twenty or thirty people whom I'd mostly never met, who were mostly musicians. Later, when some of us were outside smoking cigarettes, I shared the lyrics with a stranger I'd bonded with.

"Whoa," he said. "That's for real."

He meant it, and I felt a new sort of pride. Back then, I didn't show anyone anything. I didn't perform; I didn't even sing in my own band for months, even though I was the singer. (Why did Rob keep me around?) I was too scared, too insecure. Sharing like this was new. I was emboldened by it.

Maybe I thought the line was deep then; it means little to me now. But I felt a pull to do something with that old melody for this album, even though I can't tell you why, not really. I could come up with an explanation, sure, but that would just obscure the deeper mystery at play. The magic. The most I will say is that it felt right. Not an emotional feeling of rightness, but an instinct.

I thought the coolest way to open and close an album would be with unadorned vocals. A lyric right at the front, with just a bass note to carry it forward, and a lyric right at the end, continuing even after the drums have finished. But I didn't premeditate it. *Natural Feelings* just worked as an opener, and it just so happened to be the oldest idea on the album, and it just so happened to open with vocals only. *Precipice* just worked as an ending thematically, and it just so happened to end with vocals only. This is the magic, and why my job as an artist is to get out of the way and let The Muse do its work.

What you love is the definition of what you fear.
What you love is the definition of what you fear.
What you want, everything you can't see, everything you can't be, everything you don't need.
What you want, everything I've got until you've got me, then everything I'm not.
I can't blame you, you can't blame me, these are natural feelings.
A definition isn't what you need, but definition is what you seek.
My blood is beating my heart.
What I love, what will never be enough, going up.
What I love, what will never be enough, going up.
What I want, everything I can't see, everything I can't be, everything I don't need.
What I want, everything I've caught and no longer free, and that's where it stops.
I can't blame you, you can't blame me, these are natural feelings.
A definition doesn't set me free, in a cage looking for the key.
My blood is beating my heart.
My blood is beating my heart.
My blood is beating my heart.
My blood is beating my heart.
I'll keep looking for another
Question with no answer.
I'll keep looking for another.
I'll keep looking for another
Answer when there's no answer.
Is there love without a lover.

What you love, reach your arms out, grab what's near.

UNRAVEL

I wrote these songs for you, and they're about you, and they're about him too. Some of the songs are so blended that they could be about either one of you and still be true.

Unravel became the biggest risk. Piano and vocals only, with just a light sprinkle of synth, leaving it raw and empty. We could have dressed the song up with drums, but the one time we tried to jam it, Michael said "fuck this" and walked out, and Rob and I decided in that moment we'd record the song without him. We agreed the song would have more impact that way, in its barest and most vulnerable form. That's the truth, and it's the story we tell, but the story we don't tell is that I just didn't want to hurt Michael any more than I already had, and I had hurt him so many times, over and over again.

Both of us lose it all, lose it all.
We go, we domino.
Both of us unravel, unravel.
We know it's nothing we know.
Both of us take the fall, take the fall
We float up to the stars.
Look at us, we're not so far apart at all.
Take the distance, could we make it ours.
Take the distance, could we make it ours.
I'm sorry for the worst I've been.
Dreaming us clean in the ruins.
I'm sorry for the worst I've been.
And I'm sorry for the best,
When it goes, when it goes, when it goes

Away.
Both of us lose it all, lose it all, lose it all.
Both of us unravel, unravel, unravel,
Unravel.
Look at us, we're not so far apart at all.
Take the distance, can we make it art?
Take the distance.
I'm sorry for the worst of it.
A hundred reasons for the mess we're in.
I'm sorry for the worst of it.
And I'm sorry for the best
When it goes, when it goes, when it goes
Away.

HOSTAGE

Hostage was my problem child. There's always one, isn't there? I sent my first demo to a producer I'm friends with, and he turned it into something that wasn't right, but the problem was that I didn't know what right *was*. I just knew what right *wasn't*. We brought the song back to the drawing board and tried again.

The four of us sat down and jammed it out in the studio one afternoon, recording off the floor. It was fine enough, and I didn't want to cause trouble by being too picky, as I inevitably had been throughout the recording process. But when I heard the first mix, laying on that couch with him that summer week in Queens, I cringed through the entire play-back. It wasn't right. It sounded like a nu-metal song, a rock song. It sounded cheesy and obvious.

When I told Rob, he said, "Really? That's one of my favorites on the album." Michael said the same thing. Our recording engineer had been showing *Hostage* to friends, choosing it to spotlight among the other songs. Everyone liked it except me.

When I play *Hostage* on the piano, the left hand stays on the note "D" for the entire song, even when the right-hand chords change. It just happened that way, but I realized afterward that the song was a hostage of the note D. How perfectly fitting for a song called *Hostage*, right? Magic. The song would not – should not – get the relief of escape.

But our power-chord rock version of Hostage was predictable and not trapped by the note D. I imagined the final track as something darker and creepier, not as something Imagine Dragons would write. Even now, in the midst of our mixing process, I don't know what it'll become, but we've scrapped parts and re-recorded parts, and my hope, secret except to all of you, is that this one ends up being my proudest work on the album.

This was the only song on the album where I recorded the vocals in long, continuous single takes. There were three takes total, and the final take is a patchwork of them. Getting the right expression, detail and accuracy is much more challenging with continuous recordings, and I, being the meticulous vocalist that I am, generally prefer to create perfect short takes as opposed to imperfect longer ones. But sometimes the imperfections are what's best for the song. Loosening up the control.

If *Shiver in the Sun* is the essence of the album, then *Hostage* is the antagonist. It's the reason the conversations stay in my head, the reason for smallness and ordinariness. It's a cage of my creation, a cage of convention.

Is this love I'm a hostage of?
Memories hold the weight of the future.
Close my eyes so I can bring you closer,

Fantasies lift me out of the weather.
Falling in love like falling asleep,
With eyes wide open inside the dream.
This pain is alive and it brings you closer.
Here I'm going through the motions, killing time.
I'm fine, fucked up and fine at the same time.
Calm in the flames.
You're mine and not mine at the same time.
And nothing has changed.
Wandering around, you're a ghost in my head,
In crowded rooms and alone in my bed.
If this is love that I'm a hostage of,
Come on, open up the door for me.
Come on, open up the door for me.
Come on, open up the door for me.
I'm fine, fucked up and fine at the same time.
Calm in the flames.
You're mine and not mine at the same time.
And nothing has changed.
Open up the door for me.
Open up the door for me.
Open up the door for me.
Open up the door for me.

Hostage is also a story of the events, not just abstractions. *I'm fucked-up and fine at the same time* were actual words he said, and I captured them in my journal. Like *Unravel*, *Hostage* is about them both, and about all four of us, really. The album ends with cliff-jumping into the unknown, maybe finding freedom. This song is the reason for cliff-jumping in the first place.

It's very simple. The reason for being stuck is in waiting for someone — waiting for life — to open the door. The end of this album's journey is simply this: I'm not waiting anymore. It's time to be the god of my reality. It's time to tell a different story.

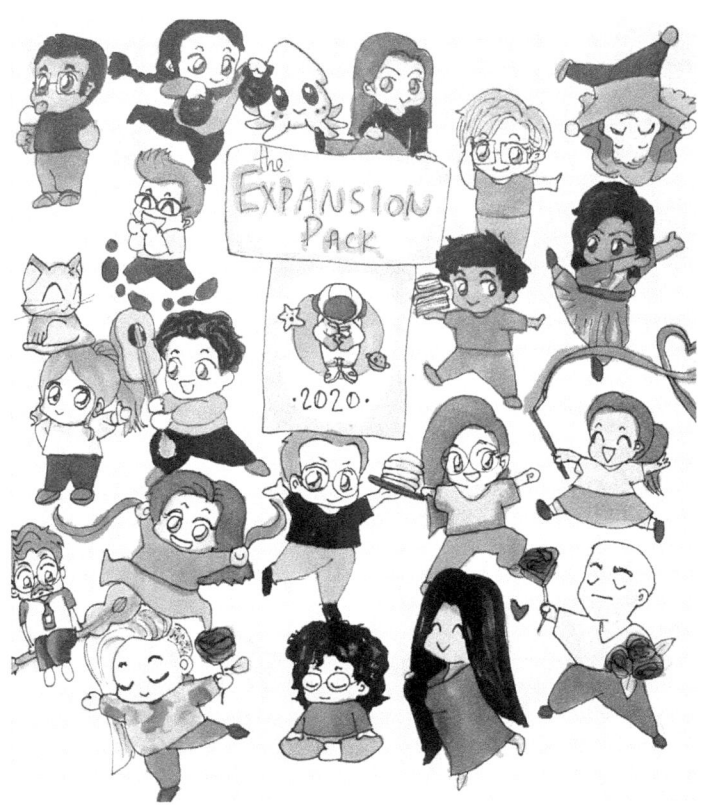

The Expansion Pack 2020 by Allysia

Have you ever dreamed of typing at the speed of thought? Have you wished you could write faster than you—or most people—talk? It turns out that you can make this a reality.

There are special keyboards that let people type at over 200 words per minute with enough practice, a feat that very few people can manage on conventional ones. The most common kind looks a bit different from what most people are used to:

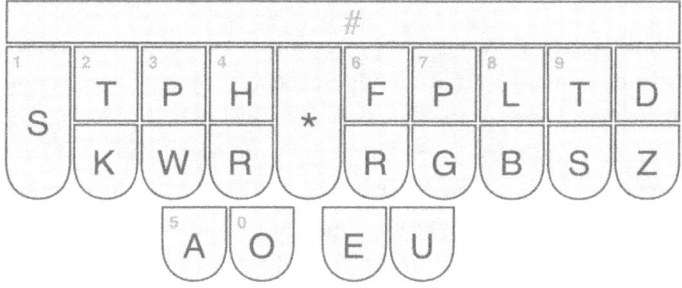

Source: https://en.wikipedia.org/wiki/File:Stenotype_en_layout.svg

Why would you want to type this fast? It lets you write as fast or faster than you can speak, and lets you make verbatim transcripts of people talking. Some countries have people recording legal cases, called "court stenographers". Some people use it as an accessibility tool, making conferences and lectures more available to deaf people and intermediate speakers of a language with real-time captioning. People even use it to flirt. https://www.youtube.com/watch?v=CD9QXrvRDZ4

How does steno let people type fast? There are a few tricks to it. One is how few keys there are: people rest most fingers between two keys. Your left thumb hovers between *a* and *o*, your left index finger between *h* and *r*, etc. Another is that you press a bunch of keys at the same time, instead of having to wait for each finger to lower and raise before the next one can strike. Lastly, you don't actually fully spell out each word: there's a system that lets you type significantly less letters than normal for the same words.

Steno was a fairly rare and unapproachable art a few years ago. Stenotype machines often cost thousands of dollars, and the software that "translates" key presses into words was similarly expensive — and people would often study steno in physical schools for a couple of years, paying hefty tuition the whole time. In 2007, a professional stenographer named Mirabai Knight started the Open Steno Project. There is now a thriving community that uses software called plover, open source textbooks and learning exercises, and hobbyist keyboards, at least some of which can stand up to sustained professional use too. You can get started for $0, and a good hobbyist keyboard is around a hundred bucks, generally under two hundred.

If you're curious, you can probably try steno right now, on your current keyboard. http://www.openstenoproject.org/

demo/ has a simple demo. If you get bitten by the bug, http://www.openstenoproject.org/ will pull you deeper. *"Learn Plover!"* is a good textbook, and *"Art of Chording"* is also popular. When you want a break from theory and to do some typing, https://didoesdigital.com/typey-type/ has your back. You may want to decrease the amount of words, or your first lessons will take a while!

The basics of steno theory are straightforward (for the type of English steno being described in this article, at least). On the left side of the keyboard, you have a bunch of consonants that are used to start words or syllables; on the right side, consonants finish them. At the bottom, you have vowels. To write "tap", you type a "t" on the left side, an "a" at the bottom, and a "p" at the right side, only letting your fingers up when you're done. To write "pat", you type a "p" on the left side, an "a" at the bottom, and a "t" on the right side. If you want to write a word like "stop", you hold down both the "s" and the "t" key on the left (as well as typing "o" and the right side's "p"). "Halts" works the same way, with "l", "t", and "s" all being held down on the right side. Simple, right?

You may be nodding, or starting to scratch your head. The whole keyboard above has 23 keys. English has at least 26 letters, even before you start doubling them. You'll only find "k" printed on the left and "z" printed on the right, and "c" "i", etc are nowhere to be found, much less "q" or "x" or "y". The next bit of theory is using combinations of keys near each other to make up for those missing letters: for example, an initial "L" is type by combining "h" and "r" on the left side. To type "let", you'd type "h" and "r" on the left, "e" at the bottom, and "t" on the right. The combinations are largely based on being fairly easy to type, and reducing the amount of times you'd want the same letter twice on the same side, because you can't use it standalone and in a combination at the same time. It's a little bit convoluted, but the underlying idea is straightforward.

These key combinations do mean that you can sometimes end up pressing most of the letters on one side at once. It's kept from becoming incredibly ambiguous by another theory concept, "steno order". Keys go from top to bottom and left to right, with the vowels between the two chunks of consonants. A mnemonic for steno order, attributed to Lars Doucet, is " **S** hould **T** he **K** ing **P** lease **W** ear **H** is **R** ed **A** nd **O** range **STAR** ry **E** lephant **U** nderwear **F** or **R** oyal **P** urposes **B** efore **L** unch **G** ets **T** otally **S** uper **D** evoured (by) **Z** ombies?"

The advantage of steno order is that it makes it clear that "r-a-p-s" is raps and not rasp. A lot of combination just don't happen in English - for instance, there are words that start with "sl" (slight), but not "ls". An "s" after the vowels is the single most annoying exception, because lots of words end with s, but lots of words also have another consonant after it. One convention is to use "f" for "s", which has several advantages, including that it is the first consonant on the right in steno order, it looks a bit like an old-fashioned s. An example of this in action is the usual way type "trust": "t-r-u-f-t", or with the usual convention without hyphens, "truft".

The other secret of steno is in reducing the amount you have to type. There are a couple of major parts to this. One is fitting more into what you can type at once: "rugd" outputs "rugged". There are a lot of words where you can ignore an unstressed vowel and effectively type two syllables at once if it doesn't conflict with another word you would otherwise type the same way. Similarly, there are key combinations for things like "-tion" that appear in a lot of words.

The other is something called "briefs", which are kind of like abbreviations. You can define any available combination of keys to output anything, no matter how long, whether it's a word or a phrase. Doing this in a way you can remember, with a system behind it, can be a little bit of an art form, but tools like plover come with a lot of predefined briefs. https://sites. google.com/site/ploverdoc/appendix-cheat-sheet has a number of common examples.

The rabbit hole goes deeper. There are several steno systems for English, and a lot for other languages, but the core concepts tend to be pretty similar. Plover is free, customizable, and proven in professional use; it's a great place to start (and stay) unless you have a strong reason to use something else.

Congratulations. If you've read this whole article, you've seen ideas that people used to be introduced to over the course of months, and if you've tried out the demo, you've taken a first step toward learning a really cool skill.

CHAPTER 13

FROM LUMPY BLOB TO LUSTROUS PEARL

BY MICHELLE MIYAGI

TODAY IS NOVEMBER 11, 2020.

I've chucked all of my ideas, goals, and plans out of the window for the rest of the year. I aim to meander and do whatever calls to me, whatever I want. This entire year has been a roller coaster with bursts of determined ambition, resulting progress, among splats of setbacks and disappointments. It has beaten me down into submission. I learned of the NaNoWriMo writing challenge in an email sent from our local library and joined on a whim. I've heard about this writing challenge for years but never took part. Well, here I go now!

I'm getting over a horrible stomach virus that began in the wee hours of the morning on my birthday Friday October 30th. I'd gotten into a nice fun new routine where I was drawing, playing guitar, dancing and making a video every day besides the daily blogging I'd pledged to do this whole year. The last 100 days of the year I'd committed to the dancing, drawing and playing guitar. I tacked on the daily video for the last 75 days of the year. I was making excellent progress and my health was returning. Wham! Sick again, sigh.

I'd gotten my flu shot the week prior and wonder if this made me more vulnerable to opportunistic infection? I probed my mind, recalling everywhere I'd been. What got me sick? Maybe it was something I ate? At first, I thought it was this cayenne vegan cheese because for the two nights prior, I had severe epigastric pain and nausea after eating it. But the next night it happened again, no cheese involved, and didn't let up. I wondered if it was my soy coffee creamer. Was it spoiled? I'd had decaf coffee each afternoon on those days. Was that the culprit?

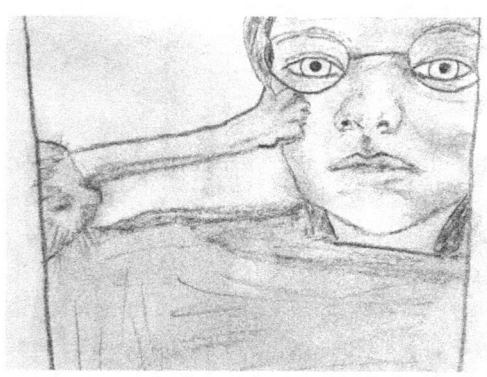

My sneaking suspicion was it might be COVID-19 again. It's possible to get it more than once. I obsessed was it from slipping my finger under my mask to get a hair out of my mouth while we were grocery shopping that Monday, or was it cooties on the grocery bags because the elderly cashier pulled her mask down, licked her fingers to help separate the plastic bags? (shudder) Had I touched my eyes or mouth while putting groceries away? Was it from my first-time glasses I'd picked up that week? Did I get it from the nurse who vaccinated me with the flu shot? I realized I would never know and gave up trying to pinpoint it.

I became incapacitated for several days; it was so painful, and I developed fever, body aches, chills and sweating, horrible cold sweats. At one point I began shivering where my teeth were chattering like a jack hammer. Better rehydrate or else I'd end up in the ER.

I called out in a weak voice to Drue my husband in the next room to please come cover me up, I'd kicked the covers to the floor and bring me water or some Clementine/Peach San Pellegrino juice flavored water, hoping it would replenish some electrolytes. Turning over I'd get on all fours to avoid using my abdominals, they were so sore and stabbing pain would shoot through me if I moved the wrong way.

I was so thankful we'd kept the cases of water and San Pellegrino that we received by mistake a few months prior. There was no way to track them, so the simplest thing was to keep them. It was much easier drinking from a bottle while I was delirious and shivering.

Drue appeared apprehensive as he covered me and placed the waters on my nightstand, asking if there was anything else he could do. I croaked out a no in between teeth chatters and drinking more water to make the shaking stop. He left the room, closing the door behind him, and resumed playing video games on the Switch in the living area. Our apartment is small with the kitchen and living area all one room connected to a balcony and the bedroom and bathroom are next to that so it's cozy.

I drank the two containers of water down and after an hour my shaking stopped. I called out again for Drue twice, but there was no response. He must have gone out to get Tylenol, which I'd wanted to take the night before, but we had none. Ibuprofen might irritate my already suffering stomach. Drue had offered the night before to go get some Tylenol after he got home from work at 11 pm, but I said no, that I'd be okay. Well, the next day I wasn't okay, I was feverish and worsening. I'd been avoiding liquids because I was in too much pain, too weak, and didn't want to move any more than necessary, which meant I dreaded having to pee.

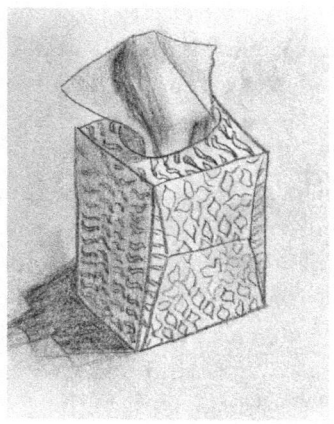

It encouraged me he'd taken initiative and was out getting things to help me. I texted him thinking he was out, and I asked him for Tylenol, Pedialyte, Popsicles and mint lip balm. The balms I had were too sweet, making me more nauseous, but my lips were so dry.

There was no response to my text, so I thought maybe he was still home and had fallen asleep, so I tried calling him. No answer. I wondered where he was and lay there helpless. Ten or fifteen minutes passed, and he entered the room apologizing his phone was on silent and saying he would go to the store. I had him bring more water before he left. He'd been playing video games and didn't hear me, but he checked his phone and saw my text.

I was thankful he was going to get the things I needed to help me avoid a trip to the ER, but it disappointed me. If the roles were reversed, I would have already googled how to help. Baby me thought he was doing the bare minimum to help me. Another part of me made excuses for him. He doesn't want to catch the illness, he's got anxiety and OCD, we socialize men that way, to view caregiving as women's work, he can't help it.

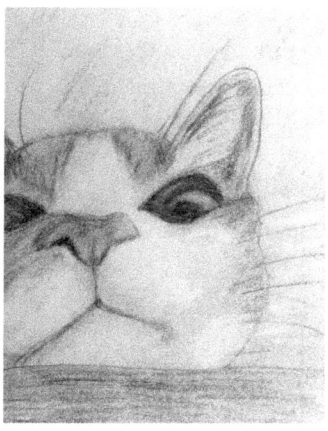

This eased my frustration somewhat, but it's common sense and human decency to do everything you can to help your loved ones when they are ill. It was mind boggling to me he was playing video games, so immersed that he didn't hear me calling out and failed to check on me when I was inches away from an ER trip and at risk for going into shock (okay a bit dramatic, lol). There's no excuse for ignorance these days with all the information available in our pockets at our fingertips. It miffed me for a bit, now I'm over it, small potatoes.

Maybe I was projecting onto Drue, my irritation with society and how some are self-centered, are defying responsibilities, who don't believe in science and worship money above human lives. It does not compute. We live in the same world, but diverge in our capabilities and perspectives, so we live in alternate realities where what makes sense to others is incomprehensible to me.

The next few days I began recuperating. I began sneezing and had a sore throat. My abdomen remained sore for days in the right upper quadrant. Could it be gallstones, or pancreatitis, or COVID? This was so severe. Could it just be a stomach bug?

A pile of bottles loomed on the floor by the bed. I dropped them, too weak to walk to the trash. The hash brown cradled me for the first days of this pesky stomach bug. We call it the hash brown because it's two futons stacked upon one another and when they are in the case, it's a bean bag couch that looks like a potato because of its tan color and oblong shape. So, when it's out of the case, it is square-ish —more like a hash brown patty.

I tossed and turned on that hash brown, lying across it the wrong way so I wouldn't veer off the edge. It was more secure for me being wedged against the top near the wall. I thrashed around in pain so much that my hair became witchy, tangled, and matted. I stayed on the futon because I didn't want to get Drue sick. And I would disturb him less when I had to rush to the bathroom to barf, though I barfed little.

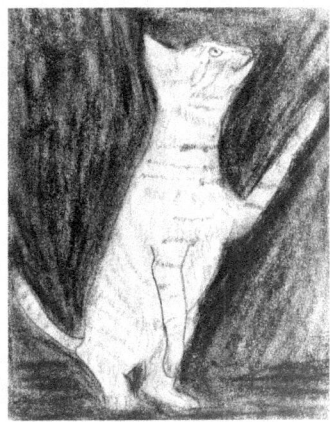

A couple of days later I got back in bed where it was more stable, not slippery and squishy like the futon. It was dark and cool in the bedroom. It hurt so much to move. Curses spewed from my mouth with each reluctant motion. I couldn't stand up straight, I was like a nursing home resident. Thoughts of how people I took care of didn't want to drink too much because they didn't want to get up to pee intruded. I understood the faulty reasoning now.

I stayed in bed. A few days later, I ventured out of my darkened lair to the living area. The light was harsh, surreal. My eyes protested. Everything appeared far away, disconnected, like there was an Instagram filter in my head making everything stark and cold. Every sound assaulted my ears, magnified, like in a David Lynch movie. Zombie-like, I stumbled around, hunched over from the soreness in my abdomen, and couldn't stay up for long. I'd spent hours drenched in cold, clammy sweat; I'd have to change my clothing multiple times. I was delirious, in and out of sleep. It was shocking and humbling to become so incapacitated, vulnerable.

There was nothing to do but endure. This year has been

shocking and humbling for us all. We accept, surrender, and endure. We make the best of it, we persevere, we help one another as best we can.

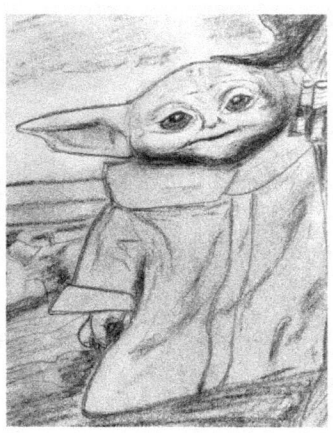

It's now December 17, 2020. I didn't finish the NaNoWriMo challenge. Post-viral syndrome as in COVID-19 long hauler's has kicked my ass since I first fell ill February 25th. The news said the coronavirus was just a mild flu happening way across the world. Then wham!

This year has kicked all of our asses. Yet, when do we learn and grow the most? It's the adversity that stretches, strengthens, expands and polishes us beyond what we can imagine. The universe is a trickster that way. We are gaining through it all, though on the surface it doesn't appear that we could have benefits from our ass-kickings.

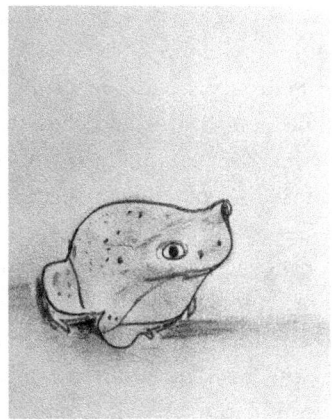

This year has me reflecting over the past decade that has led me to now. All the challenges I'd thought were too difficult, that there was little chance I could make it to where I wanted to go. Frustration, being stuck, not knowing what to do, or how to do it. All the grasping, seeking, grieving, struggling, striving to make sense of it all, while enjoying, appreciating, sharing, growing, exploring, experimenting, thriving. It's a wild, wondrous life, ass-kickings and all.

I believe we all are being tested by this pandemic in ways we never could have predicted. It's a global reckoning of sorts. Adversity reveals what lies beneath, it's like a membrane being stretched over it all until everything pokes through the surface into the light of day. Then our genuine work begins where it's all out in the open, the truth, warts and all.

I've written about my experience with the rollercoaster of long haulers syndrome in daily blog posts this year. I'd think I was better, then I'd increase my activities, then relapse, within a week. My symptoms improved over the months, and I had to forgo exercise or strenuous activities. Then I would test it by increasing my activity. If I relapsed, I'd decrease my activity again. It's my year of the lumpy blob, me. Maybe it's the world's year of lumpy blobness too?

At the end of February, I had an awful cold, along with a trigger finger and hand rash. With subsequent relapses I have had sinus/chest congestion, hand rash, shortness of breath, tachycardia/palpitations, cold hands/feet/nose, feet so cold they hurt, migraines w/auras, less severe headaches, ashen complexion/lips, eye inflammation and severe fatigue, light-headedness with brain fog. Over the summer until now these symptoms trailed off until there was just sinus/chest congestion, headaches, hand rash, intermittent shortness of breath, mild tachycardia, mild fatigue, eye inflammation and cold feet during relapses.

There was no testing for non-hospitalized people, so I don't have definitive proof it was the virus, but based on everything, I'm certain it was. I had traveled by airplane from Denver to Sacramento and back in the days prior to the illness. Plus, I worked in a crowded hotel breakfast buffet. Cooties galore! Also, I've been shedding since the stomach bug, it fills my hairbrush with at least twice as much as usual and I've had to vacuum more, ewww! I had Drue check me for bald spots! None so far, whew!

I have another health issue called MdDS, Mal de Debarquement syndrome. I went on my one and only cruise in November 2015 and it's like I've never left the boat. It's a neurological ocular-vestibular disorder where I'm off balance, among other symptoms. My body adjusted to the rocking of the boat and never reset to being on steady land. Illness exacerbates the MdDS, so it's been something.

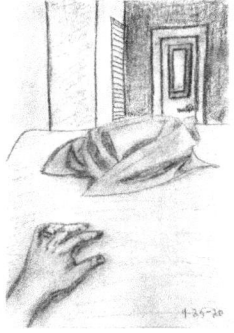

The end of February, an Uncle who was like a father to me died. I was so thankful to visit him then to say goodbye. I couldn't say goodbye though, it was too much. Instead, I said goodnight, I love you so much and sweet sleep giving kisses on the forehead because it was bedtime. All the goodbyes I witnessed; the sobbing was heart wrenching. I didn't want to put us through that. I could cry later. He was the youngest in the large family. It sucks. It was cruel and hard, yet breathtaking, the tenderness, grace and outpouring of love. Hearts flailing open wide in honor and reverence of his beautiful journey. I was so honored to be there. We all miss him so much.

He came in spirit a few days after he left this world to tell me he was doing fine in the dimension where we go when we don't have these bodies. I was holding hands with Drue. We were on the hash brown chatting in the few minutes before he left for work. The lightness, buzzing, sparkling, effervescence like a tinkling, fluttering in the center of me happened, and I heard him in my mind saying he loved me, that everything was okay, joy pervaded. It reassured and comforted me. I smiled through teary eyes, verklempt. I've had other people visit me that way after they've died. It sounds weird and unreal, but I experienced it.

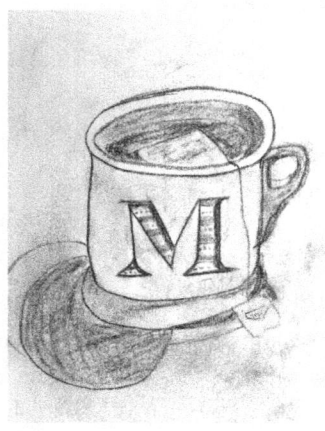

He and his husband, along with another beloved uncle, aunt and cousin had visited me the summer before. What an honor and treat. I was so loved. I know it was thanks to my uncle's spectacular husband; he coordinated everything, making sure we got to enjoy while everyone was healthy. I never knew how sick my uncle was until then. In retrospect, I wish I'd been able to have the means and opportunity to visit with them more or made different choices way back when I was just starting out in my adult life. Like moving to California to be near them. I always wanted to but was too afraid and ill equipped to do something so bold on my own.

Then comes March and we know it's serious, the coronavirus is turning into a pandemic. Oprah's 2020 Vision Tour on the 7th was an awesome experience. Little did I know it was a last hurrah. On the 17th, I get laid off from my job. I'd transitioned out of nursing in December 2019, working at Starbucks, Macy's and King Soopers bakery over a few weeks.

Then in January I landed the host job, which is a two-minute walk from me, and quit the others.

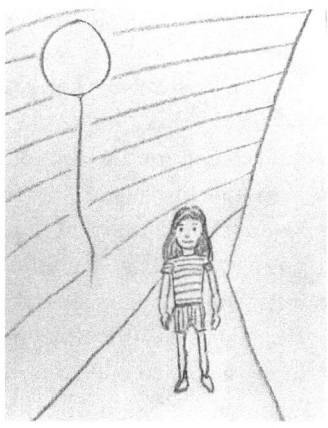

Twenty-seven years invested in nursing, but I burned out. Suicidal thoughts intruded before every shift I worked as a night nurse at a nursing home. My days off, I was fine. My conscience overruled, and I could not take part in that system anymore. Because it's a business, patients suffer because money is priority and they cut corners with the disadvantaged bearing the brunt. It was heartbreaking. In order to afford the decrease in pay with the new job, we'd moved to a cheaper apartment above us. We love this place more!

We're then on lockdown. I'm a target because I'm of Asian descent and now people fear me because of "The Chinese Virus." Since we elected Trump, I've encountered more open hostility. People fear catching coronavirus from me, so I wear a mask outdoors while walking, even though it's not required.

My mind makes plans to work out, get fit, work on projects, build a business which has been my dream for ages while we're sidelined by the pandemic. Early on, I bought hand weights and a stability ball. I did Denise Austin's Shrink Your Female Fat Zones workout once, had my first relapse, and haven't used them since.

It hasn't dawned yet back then I have post-viral syndrome. I wonder if it's all in my head when I think I'm better: go full throttle and then get sick again. OTC meds help a little. It will take repetition with mounting frustration until I see the pattern and investigate further. A Covid long haulers support group shows me that in comparison, my symptoms are not so severe. I dodged a bullet. It sobers me by recognizing I survived while so many haven't.

It's a relief, I qualify for unemployment. They offer health insurance during a special open enrollment in May for people impacted by the virus, I sign up. Got a checkup with PCP, they run labs and say I'm okay, they order nothing for my symptoms, and they don't know how to treat MdDS. They oblige when I ask for a prescription med that's helped me in the past for allergies.

I then see specialists, one for the MdDS and an allergist for my post viral flare-ups. PT and a med for the MdDS helps. I'm still doing the daily PT on my own and we're increasing the medicine again. The MdDS will go away soon, I hope. I increased OTC allergy meds, and it helps. After I healed from the stomach bug, I increased my activity and relapsed again. I go for a breathing test next week and will see the allergist again. All of my visits are virtual, except for the PT over 3 visits that I've completed.

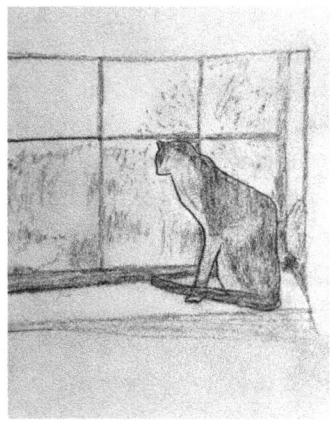

In between, I attempt to make progress on goals in my life. I have time, but my health has sucked. It's confounding and I look for the silver linings. Time to play detective and discover the hidden benefits, finding all the things we're grateful for. Gratitude and appreciation are soothing balms. What is this teaching me? How is this helping us? We, our family, are doing well despite the pandemic and marvel that everything works out after all. The illness is my body's way of getting me to slow down and rest. So, I obey it instead of forcing it to obey me. Instead of mind over matter, I surrender to my body. At first, I resist with consternation, petulance, and pity parties. My inner brat bubbles up. Since this last relapse, I've embraced restoration mode. I surrender, you wicked Covid!

Then I make friends with adversity, embracing the here and now. What else is there to do? It's only common sense to accept the things you cannot change. Resistance is futile. There is no definitive roadmap to guide us through this. We're all in a dance of improvisation together. Somehow, we persevere by helping each other get from one day to the next.

At the beginning we were all in shock and handling it in unique ways, trying to discern what was true and predict how our lives would unfold in the pandemic's wake. We dug deep, pulling out all the coping skills in our toolboxes. There were oodles of unknowns. It was unprecedented in our lifetimes and out of our control. We took to the internet in droves, seeking facts, connection, support, and validation. We were regaining our footing with each nugget of unfolding knowledge. How to reconfigure our new realities, where do we go from here?

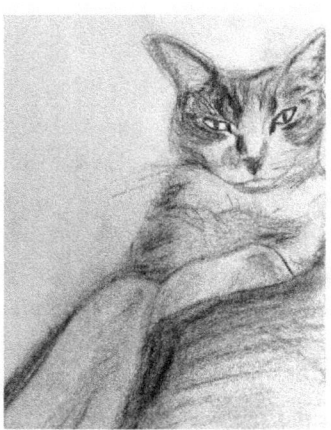

Our routine shattered and the ghost of the virus haunted us. No one could tell us for certain how contagious it was, or what to expect. This inability to pin it down caused some of us to cower in fear and others to dismiss it outright. We didn't know what to believe and have suffered for it. The pandemic remains out of control in the United States. It's worse than ever. They cannot roll the vaccine out fast enough. Many more will suffer and die. This is the grim truth. Sadness hovers around us all.

Over these months, I watched people live streaming on social media like I'd never seen. Everyone reaching out, sharing, attempting to bond, hoping to help bridge the gaping holes left by our new pandemic reality. We danced, we sang, we wrote, we drew, painted, and created. We expressed our concerns and cheered each other on. Other parts of the world showed us the ways to help, and we followed suit.

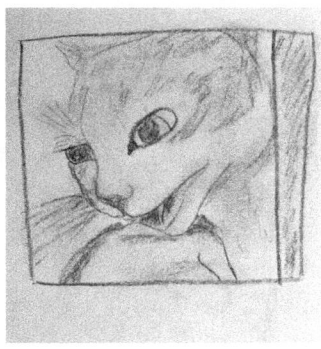

We're stripped down to what matters most. The threat of the virus made everything more precious. We take nothing for granted. There was no way to avoid ourselves. The places we turned to for distraction were not available anymore. We improvised and began baking, playing board games, crafting, spending quality time with those we live with. The great outdoors became a refuge, where we could escape from the confines of our homes. We cheered and howled from our windows and balconies for those on the frontline. Each person contributing in their own ways, spreading their good intentions, lighting the way until we get to the end of this together.

The months have warped by. Time is amorphous. What day is it today? I try to fantasize and visualize to help me cope, but it only reminds me of how confined we are still. It's dragging on forever; I can't help but admit. It's been uncomfortable and we're concluding that there's no right way to grieve, or cope with it all. Most of us have given up on convincing others to follow precautions or arguing about conspiracy theories and politics. Hunkering down is our best bet.

Isolation takes a toll. The Skype and FaceTime sessions with the kids are a lifeline. Technology, where would we be without it? I empathize with all the parents who are juggling kids with school and work from home. I can't fathom the grief from the deaths by Covid. It's overwhelming.

Acceptance settles my soul. Letting go of what I can't control saves me. We sacrifice to save more lives. So what if we can't eat at a restaurant? Can we put a price on a life? Though I worry if they don't help people facing hunger and homelessness. Something's gotta give.

Here we are, still faced with unknowns. Congress is battling it out over relief efforts, it's down to the wire. We wait.

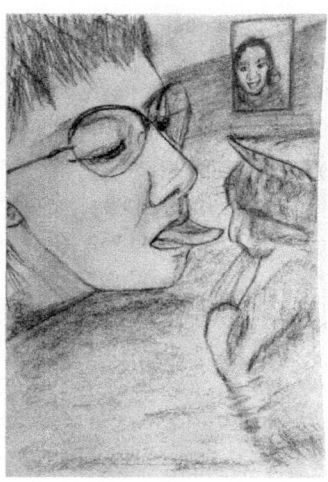

What have I learned and how have I grown this year? It's not clear yet. Ask me in a year from now. One thing I learned is I base my self-worth on accomplishments. This year I've found I don't have to earn my keep through my achievements because I've survived while being at home. I did not work or build a business, and we're fine. I've had to limit activity yet lost a few pounds. I stayed home except for grocery shopping and don't mind it. It's down to the basics here, food, roof, breathing. We're good.

Self-care has been lacking over this past decade, so this has been an opportunity for me, with this time at home. I've been able to rest and cleaned up my diet, the best I've done ever! I've adapted by bringing nature to me. I planted a balcony garden, grew celery and wheatgrass on my kitchen counter.

When I was able, I went on long nature walks. Twice we made it to a hiking trail at the nearby foothill parks. I engaged online with kindred spirits for social support. We may feel alone, but there is always someone to reach out to, always. I did workbooks on writing, self- discovery, business and began online courses towards building a business. I journaled, medi-tated, and read/listened to books. With streaming TV and movies, plus video games, we have all the creature comforts.

Beyond the sorrow, I found beauty every day. By paying attention, I discovered I am cradled in it. Overall, this time has been healing for me.

There were moments, too many, where despair ruled. It never lasts, no emotion ever lasts if we allow them to flow, they vaporize faster. Survivor's guilt reminiscent of the times of floods and hurricanes we lived through in Louisiana caught me unawares. How could I dare to indulge in negativity when others have it so much worse? There was this impulse to do everything possible to help, while I knew I was at full capacity in taking care of myself. So, I wrote in my blog, maybe sharing would help somehow, and I did my best to help anyone who reached out to me.

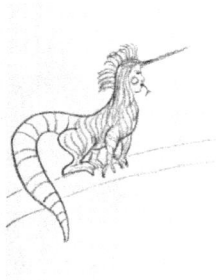

Many emotions have coursed through me, like outrage at irresponsible behavior and helpless resignation, knowing there's nothing I can do about it. When people didn't behave in ways I believed were appropriate, I learned to shelve my judgment. Judging others is not helpful for me or anyone else. I didn't have to like what they were doing, or take part, or approve, but that didn't make them lesser than or unworthy. It's better to disengage and let people be. If they are not crossing my boundaries, or causing harm that I can stop, it's none of my business. My boundaries are more defined, which brings me greater peace.

Solitude has shown me I can find peace and happiness with what's in my direct experience, in being present and mindful, there's a place inside where it's timeless and a wellspring of infinite love. It's accessible by going within. Practice during this pandemic time has strengthened my ability to be present and at peace.

In navigating this year, I've been leaning on gratitude and appreciation to rescue me from the doldrums. It works.

Looking back to all the times I've weathered stressful situations and prevailed has helped me when catastrophic thoughts spiral me into anxious fear. A favorite thought is that I've made it to now, chances are I can make it through whatever comes my way. That's why I've conjured up things I've overcome in this past decade to show me how far I've come. It gives me a reality check and boosts my confidence. In contrast, my life is stellar now, pandemic or not. This year has honed my coping skills in innumerable ways, but what will it be like when the world open backs up? We'll be jumping for joy, yet there may be some culture shock at first. We will not return to the world we had before.

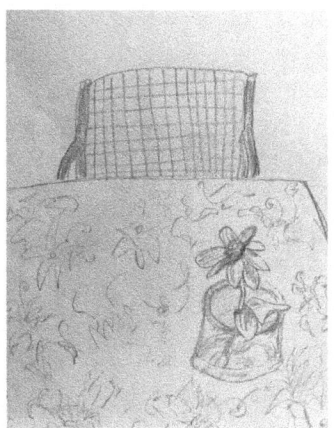

What I've learned most of all is to honor every part of me, the unwanted, the needy, the whiny assed bitching, the frightened, the smallness, the negative, and the gracious, the loving, the generous, the silly, the giddy, the adoring, the positive... the dark and light, all of it is there for my benefit. I am learning to work with myself, not against and use it all to my advantage. Parts of me I used to disavow, I now allow and embrace. Only with awareness and acceptance can I change anything. And the same goes for changing the world.

I'd say we are aware of a whole heck of a lot more than a year ago or four years ago. It's time for massive change, don't y'all think? The pandemic is revealing where there is the greatest need.

I'm feeling less and less like a lumpy blob. My goal for this year was to transform from a lumpy blob into a lustrous pearl. Well, it's taking longer than that, but all that matters to me is transformation is happening. We are in motion, growing and flowing along with the world. I can nurture the process by tuning in, listening, and partnering with myself and the universe. This year I've become my very best friend in the unlikeliest of times. Maybe we as a collective can become better friends with ourselves, each other, and the universe, and have a lustrous pearl of a world thanks to what we've learned and sown in this 2020 lumpy blob of a year.

'TIS THE SEASON OF GIVING, right?

Don't worry, even though there is a pandemic, we haven't lost the opportunity to give the most important gifts of all.

Let us start by giving to ourselves.

I'll go first.

Here is what I am giving myself:

I give myself permission to let go of the black bound journal that I lost in the flood.

I have been using the loss of that journal as an excuse for not writing, reflecting, philosophizing or introspecting in prose, for years.

It's entirely irrational, of course. Like so much of human behavior.

It wasn't a recent flood, and it wasn't a hurricane, and it wasn't a massive loss like those that so many others have suffered in the intervening years in the world. It was 10 years ago, and it was four feet of water in the basement. I remember watching boxes that I hadn't touched in months or years float to the surface, release their contents, and swirl around the open concrete oversized bathtub that the basement had become, like memories in a semi-lucid dream.

I don't remember much about anything else that I lost — I remember many philosophy books from my time in graduate school, with their margins filled with my ingenue insights and tangential thoughts, but along with the books written by others, this one, written by me. I remember fishing it out of the muddy water and opening it for the first time in so many years, and trying to determine whether it could be salvaged. The ink was bleeding, and the words were becoming even more unintelligible than they were in my original handwriting.

The whole reason that the black book was lost in the flood is because it was buried in the basement in some box with all the other philosophy books from my graduate school days, so … for at least five years, it had been down there, neglected, closed, keeping its own secrets. I wonder how many pages were even written in. I'm sure my memories have inflated the loss.

It's been ten years, and yet, I haven't ever really let it go. I have held on so strongly to all the "if only-s":

If only I still had those ideas I had written down.

If only I still had a window into my past.

If only I still had the spark of insight that I had then.

Everything would be different?

That's the logical implication of my thinking, but I know that's insane. Nothing would be different. Nothing except my excuses. I'm sure I would have thought of another one in this one's stead.

The only thing I can remember, aside from my tiny hand-writing filling every nook and cranny of the pages, loads of non-sequiturs scrawled in moments of enlightenment, and lots of stream-of-consciousness, is the idea that formed the basis of my grad school thesis — the idea counterfactual conditional.

Wikipedia explains that "a counterfactual conditional is a conditional containing an if-clause which is contrary to fact." That we, as humans with abstract language, can have such thoughts and articulate such propositions … "if only the black book hadn't been lost in the flood…" sets us up for so much pain and suffering. Because the truth about the counterfactual conditional is that whatever comes after the "if" clause is by-definition unknowable.

It's entirely speculation.

It's wild supposition.

It's literally contrary to what actually happened, so we do not know, and *yet*, we are able to (at least structurally) talk about it as though we might be accurate in our speculation.

I knew then that the seemingly dry, logical proposition that a counterfactual conditional cannot be proven is the reason why life for logical human beings is so ever-loving screwed up sometimes.

Because we think we know.

We think we know what would have happened, "if only". Or if we don't explicitly think we know what would have happened, "if only", we *act* like we think we know what would have happened, by implication. See, for example, my long-held feelings of loss over some damn notebook from decades ago. The necessary presumption that I am making is that I know how life would have turned out "if only" the notebook hadn't been lost.

It would have been better.

I would have written more.

I wouldn't have felt lost.

I would have done more.

But here is the truth: I didn't *not* lose the journal in the flood. I can't, don't, and will never know what would have happened "if only."

And it's not just a black book in which we lay such vague hopes, losses, resentments, wishes, and blame.

How many times have you thought, "if only"?

If only my husband would have done X, I would be happier.

If only I had said something different, my relationship

would be better.

If only the boss had seen more of my talents, I would have gotten the promotion.

If only my mother or father hadn't yelled or drank or died or left or loved me too much or too little, my life would have been different.

Here's the dirty little secret: these thoughts obscure *lies*.

Lies we tell ourselves to get out of taking responsibility for however our life turned out. Lies we tell ourselves to avoid dealing with the choices we have made with what we were given. Lies that keep us feeling safe in our actual victimhood, lies that leave us outside the sphere of agency, delegating our happiness, satisfaction and joy to a hypothetical past that *did. not. happen.*

So, enough.

Enough of that BS.

So, today, I give myself permission to let that go.

I accept responsibility for the fact that some notebook from ten or twenty years ago is not relevant to my current success.

I let it go.

I release my attachment to that excuse, while we are at it, to anything and everything that I might subtly believe I don't have, in order to do what I want to do with my life.

I have everything that I need.

And so do you.

Sometimes giving something up is the best gift you can give, to you and to the people you love.

What will you give up this holiday season?

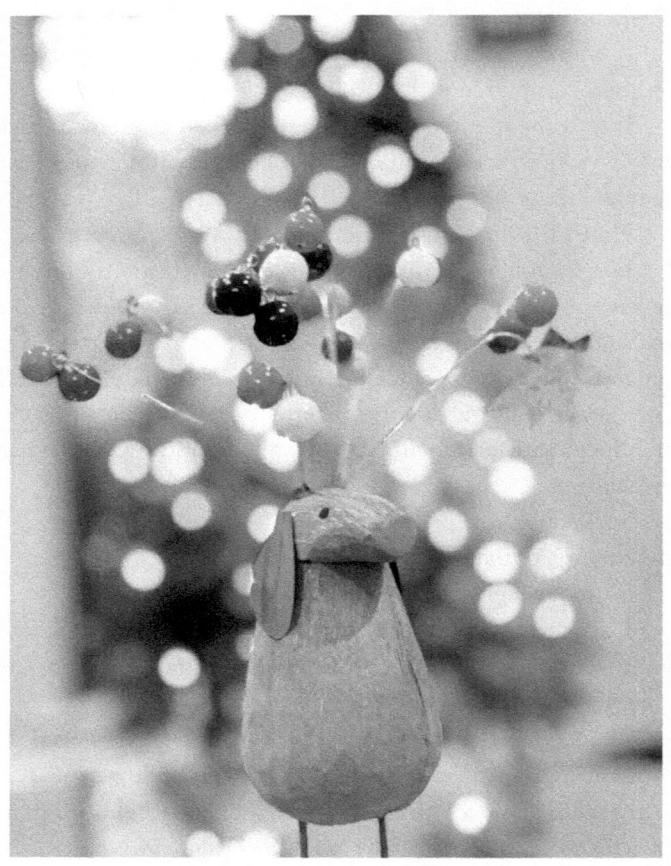

Rainbow Tree in B&W by Lauren & Kelly Roberts

It's an Easter Egg hunt!

Congratulations!

You have found a sweet little sleeping dragon.

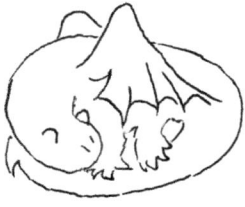

Dragon Sketch by Helen F.

Can you find the other two?

CHAPTER 15

I GOT INTO A FIGHT WITH MY WIFE IN LONDON

BY KELLY ROBERTS

IT HAPPENED IN LONDON, pre-pandemic, when we spent the majority of our time traveling and working from around the world. It happened in London, but it could have happened anywhere. We are sitting on the couch in our AirBnB flat and I am working on a graphic design project when Lauren asks me several questions about how I'm going about doing what I'm doing, and she ends with: "Why would you do it that way?"

My internal reaction to her questioning is immediate. I begin running through a list of justifications and defenses for my actions. My weapons are drawn and defenses raised, before I am even aware of what is happening.

This isn't a loud, demonstrative, or obviously argumentative fight. My mother trained me early and often—by force of switch, ruler, belt, and hand—that talking back is not an option. No, this is character assassination by sniper, perpetrated in the mind, utilizing my arsenal of stored up petty wrongs and grievances, which I have been cataloguing for this exact purpose.

I answer her with an attempt to deflect the conversation: "I'm doing it this way because I'm doing it this way."

She gets up from the couch and goes about her business. I sit there and ostensibly continue working, but now I'm using jerky and exaggerated movements, as if to assert my righteousness. Externally, I'm quiet and appear focused on my computer, but the exterior calm belies my internal turmoil.

I take Lauren's questioning my actions as an impugnment of my intelligence, decision-making ability, and manhood. I interpret Lauren's intention as accusatorial and not inquisitive. I feel like I am being told that I've done something wrong. Suddenly, in my mind, we are at odds, and not on the same team, so I feel distance between us. My mindset turns adversarial and I begin to view all of our interactions through this new lens. I continue working, doing it the way I am doing it, armed and ready to combat any future hostile infiltration.

I sit there, walled off emotionally, my ego feeling superficially protected. I get to be right, and there is a certain rush of being in battle mode, as I start tabulating all the ways that I am being unjustly injured.

My posture of justification and defensiveness causes me to withdraw further and further into myself, taking me out of the current moment of life and isolating me within the dank cellar of my mind, where I take counsel and comfort from the corpses of real and imagined injustices of the past.

The energy that is generated by this self-righteous indignation is not a creative force. It does nothing to forward what I am out to create in life. At best, it is a distraction from my ability to enjoy life and create the world I want. This energy creates distance, separation and loneness. At worst, it is the beginning of a slow dissolution of my ability to feel love and affinity for the person I love the most in this world.

The weight and pain of recasting my friend and lover as

my betrayer and adversary suppresses my joy, my self-expression, and my power. If I allow it, another layer of scar tissue will form from this self-inflicted wound, eventually becoming an impenetrable armor of distrust, self-justification, and isolation.

Can you relate? Assuming you are human, too, I imagine that you can.

So, what do I do, and what can you do, if you do not want separation to creep into your relationships? How can you prevent it from happening, especially when starting down the path is an automatic response that begins before we are even aware it's occurring?

The first step is to pay attention to your moods and behaviors and to be honest about them, with yourself and others. Being honest takes work and constant practice for me.

As soon as you realize that you are creating separation between yourself and someone you love, give up the right to defend yourself and let go of the intoxicating rush of being justified in your anger.

I take a deep breath. Or several. This calms my body and breaks the flow of negative thoughts.

Recreate what you are committed to having the relationship be like. Paint a mental picture of how you actually want it to be, and experience the positive emotions associated with that vignette. Make the choice for it to be that way, NOW!

Ask yourself: if your relationship was exactly how you want it to be, right this moment, how would you act? What thoughts about your partner would you have? What would you say? What would you do? Take full responsibility for your actions and words. Give up being the victim. Clean up anything you need to with the other person.

This is not about you putting up with either physical, mental, or verbal abuse. Sometimes taking responsibility looks like setting boundaries, and not allowing the other person to violate their own integrity and humanity by treating you in certain ways. That may mean ending abusive relationships.

What this is about is you standing in your own power, irrespective of the actions of others. This is about you creating and living the life of your design and not surviving an automatic and reactionary life.

Within the hour of realizing that I was creating separation, I shifted my thoughts and behaviors back to love and affinity for Lauren. A fight that would have lasted for days early on in our relationship, never had time to fester or grow into a lasting barrier between us.

The next day we enjoyed the Queen's Walk and ended the day watching the sunset at Big Ben. Together.

You hold the power to make your relationships great.

Will you create wonderful memories or breed anger and resentment?

The choice is yours.

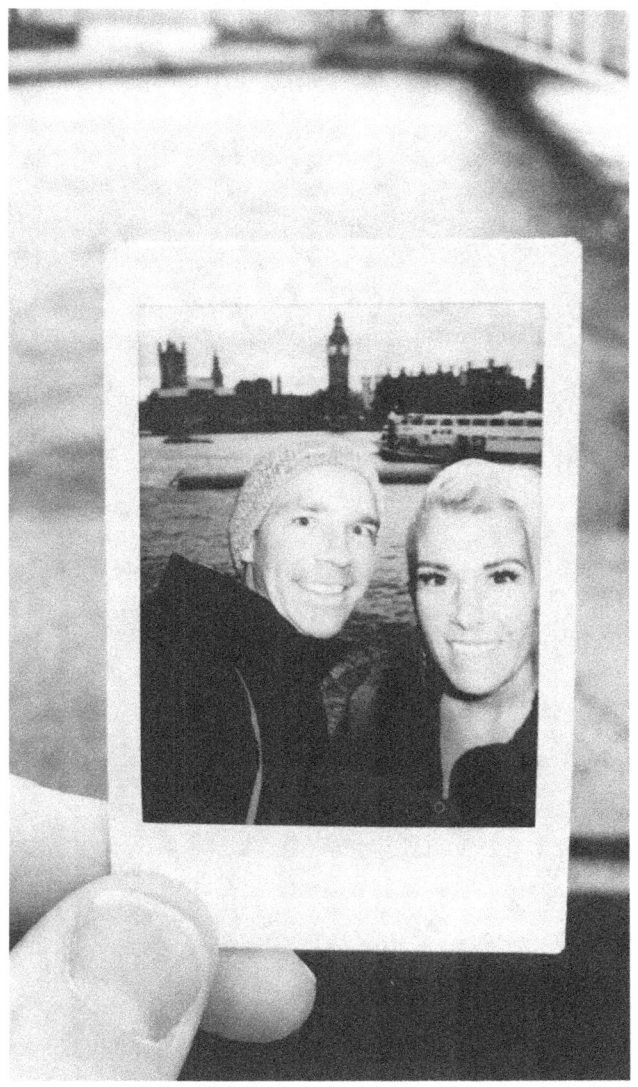

Photo of Photo of Kelly & Lauren by Kelly Roberts

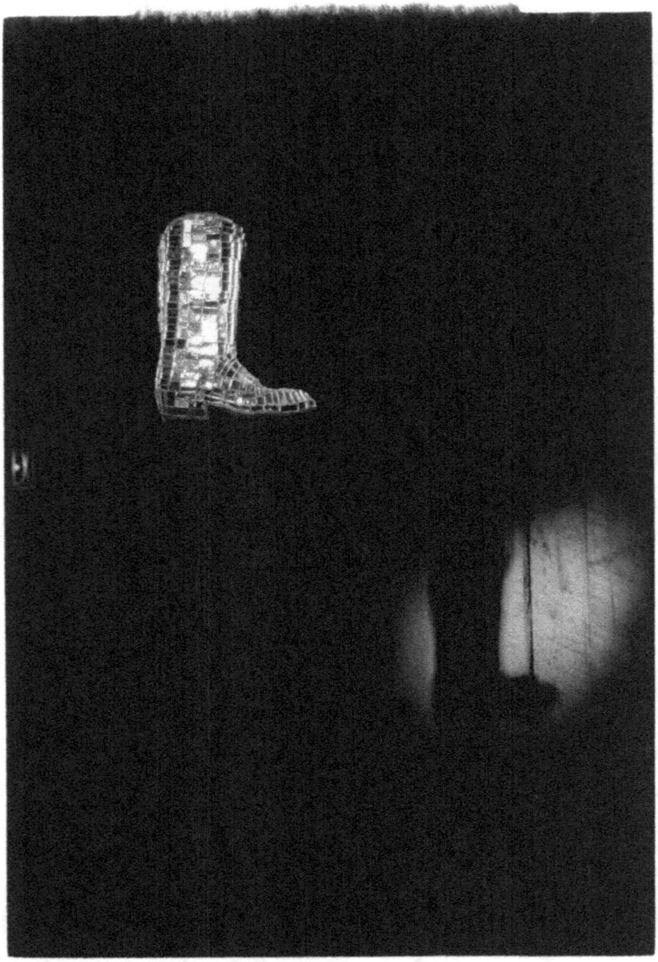

Urban Disco by Kelly Roberts

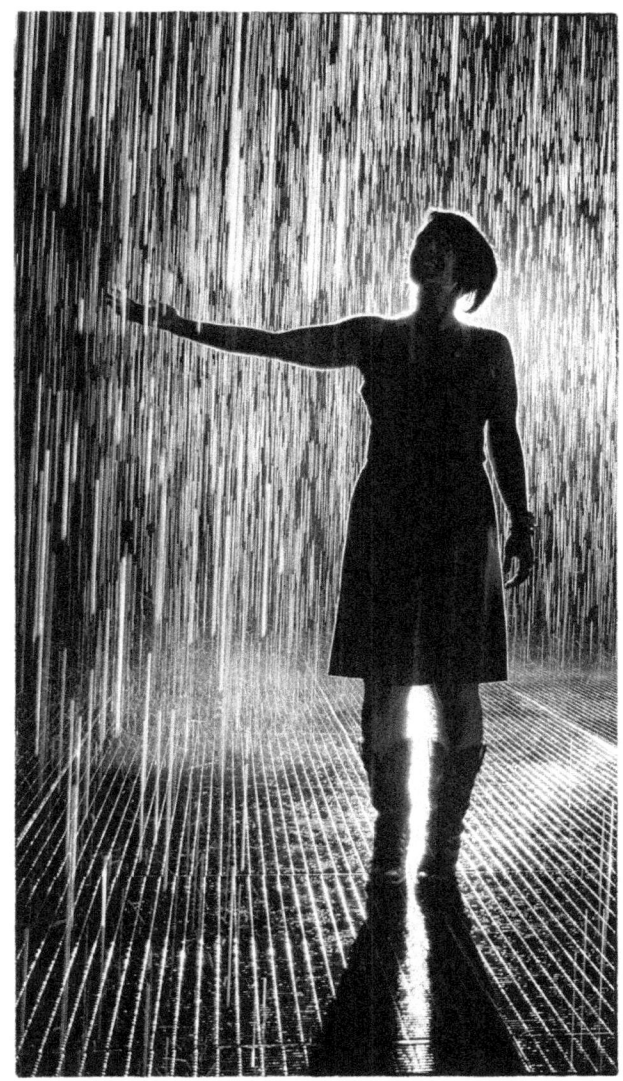

Lauren in the Rain Room, NYC by Kelly Roberts

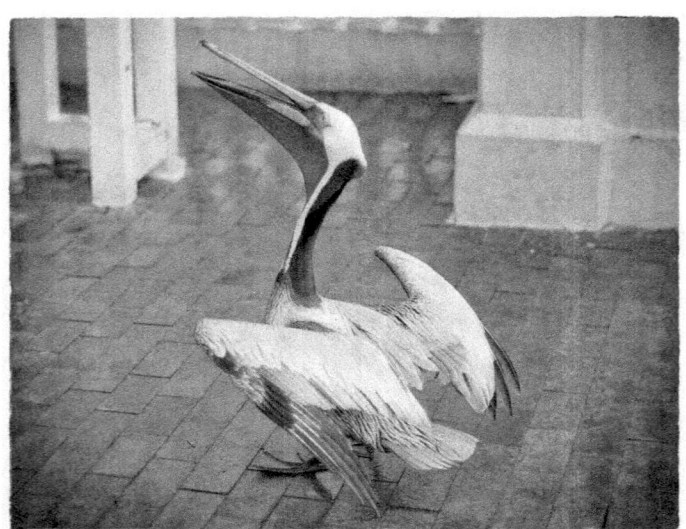

Pelican in St. Petersburg by Kelly Roberts

ACKNOWLEDGMENTS

This book is the collective creation of an amazing group of people who have come together in *The Expansion Pack.*

Thank you to everyone who submitted, and may the best for all of us be yet to come.